Beyond Snakes and Shamrocks

Beyond Snakes and Shamrocks

St. Patrick's Missional Leadership Lessons for Today

Ross A. Lockhart

FOREWORD BY
Darrell L. Guder

CASCADE *Books* · Eugene, Oregon

BEYOND SNAKES AND SHAMROCKS
St. Patrick's Missional Leadership Lessons for Today

Copyright © 2018 Ross A. Lockhart. All rights reserved. Except for brief quotations in critical publications or reviews, no part of this book may be reproduced in any manner without prior written permission from the publisher. Write: Permissions, Wipf and Stock Publishers, 199 W. 8th Ave., Suite 3, Eugene, OR 97401.

Cascade Books
An Imprint of Wipf and Stock Publishers
199 W. 8th Ave., Suite 3
Eugene, OR 97401

www.wipfandstock.com

PAPERBACK ISBN: 978–1-5326–3497–0
HARDCOVER ISBN: 978–1-5326–3499–4
EBOOK ISBN: 978–1-5326–3498–7

Cataloguing-in-Publication data:

Names: Lockhart, Ross A., author. | Guder, Darrell L., foreword.

Title: Beyond snakes and shamrocks : St. Patrick's missional leadership lessons for today / Ross A. Lockhart.

Description: Eugene, OR: Cascade Books, 2018 | Includes bibliographical references.

Identifiers: ISBN 978–1-5326–3497–0 (paperback) | ISBN 978–1-5326–3499–4 (hardcover) | ISBN 978–1-5326–3498–7 (ebook)

Subjects: LCSH: Patrick, Saint, 373?–463? | Mission of the church—Canada. | Mission of the church—United States. | Christianity—21st century.

Classification: BV2070 .L4 2018. (print) | BV2070 .L4 (ebook)

Scripture quotations marked NRSV are taken from the Holy Bible, New Revised Standard Version Bible, copyright 1989, Division of Christian Education of the National Council of the Churches of Christ in the United States of America. Used by permission. All rights reserved. Scripture quotations marked (NIV) are taken from the Holy Bible, New International Version®, NIV®. Copyright © 1973, 1978, 1984, 2011 by Biblica, Inc.™ Used by permission of Zondervan. All rights reserved worldwide. www.zondervan.com The "NIV" and "New International Version" are trademarks registered in the United States Patent and Trademark Office by Biblica, Inc.™ Scripture quotations marked THE MESSAGE. Copyright © by Eugene H. Peterson 1993, 1994, 1995, 1996, 2000, 2001, 2002. Used by permission of Tyndale House Publishers, Inc.

Manufactured in the U.S.A.   06/29/18

For Emily, Jack, and Sadie,
a threefold blessing
from our Triune God.

Contents

Foreword

Darrell L. Guder

"PARADIGM SHIFT" HAS BECOME a much used term in conversations about the rapid and radical changes that continue to shape Western cultures. The term is useful because the subject matter of these conversations has become so complex and multi-dimensional. For the sake of cogent communication, we need a term that summarizes what is going on. The concept of "paradigm" appears to capture the vast structural shape of this passage of cultural change. The basic frameworks of Western thought and practice are not only under review, they are profoundly threatened and are being replaced by entirely new sets of assumptions to guide our sense of who we are and where we are in the adventure of Western cultures. Until very recently, we could talk about "Western culture" and "Christian culture" and assume that we were talking more or less about the same thing. The dominant paradigm, after centuries of a history we describe as Christendom, privileged the Christian faith. Every aspect of Western culture was profoundly shaped by the shared legacy of Christianity. The language about the emerging paradigms that are rapidly replacing hegemonic Christendom focuses on terms like secularization, post-Christianity or post-Christendom, rationalism, progress, globalization, enlightenment, humanism, skepticism, and reliance upon science. There is no question that Bonhoeffer was right when he recognized that contemporary Western cultures see themselves as having come "of age" and now capable of consciously moving beyond the intellectual and culture immaturity of pre-modernity. Of the paradigms available, the inherited assumptions of Christianity are widely dismissed as no longer viable. The "snakes and shamrocks" of fifth-century Ireland are relics of a closed chapter, for which the paradigm of modernity has no place.

This comprehensive process of paradigm shift has, of course, radically reshaped the Christian mission. With the disintegration of the structures and stances of Christendom, the purpose of the Christian movement has been subjected to intense scrutiny. The outcome, for much of the intellectual establishment of the West, has been the unquestioned consensus that Christendom is over. Whatever the Christian mission was about in earlier centuries, it is no longer germane today. What is needed are new paradigms that focus upon the human capacity to address all challenges of life and survival on our planet. The intellectual world of Western modernity is generating a whole spectrum of such paradigms that are predominantly negative about the Christian legacy and its alleged mission.

This means that the interpreters of that mission today face a daunting task when they continue to claim that the events surrounding the person of Jesus Christ in the middle East in the first century of the "common era" are as revolutionary and powerful now as they were then. The Christian witnesses of that first century confronted hostile paradigms when they began to cross borders and share their message with more and more cultures of their day. They grappled with the scorn and derision of the dominant paradigm then, just as followers of Christ do today. The paradigms generated by human societies then and now are rarely cordial to the biblical message; they are challenged by it.

Going back to its initiation in the first century, the Christian mission has been guided by the first Christians' conviction that their purpose was defined by the words of their ascending Lord: "You shall be my witnesses in Jerusalem, Judea, Samaria, and to the ends of the earth" (Acts 1:8). The original company of Christian missionaries were graduates of the Rabbi Jesus' school for disciples, learners of Jesus, who discovered after Easter that their vocation was to be his "sent ones"—apostles. Their sentness meant that they were constantly challenging the dominant paradigms of their context because Jesus Christ was Lord—and no other. This made them necessarily bi-cultural: they lived in the basic paradigm of God's inbreaking reign in Jesus Christ. And they were called and sent to be evidence of that reign in a world profoundly opposed to such a message. Their witness centered on their translation of the truth of the biblical paradigm into cultural contexts defined by opposing paradigms.

Ross Lockhart is assuming the end of Christendom and the challenges of radical paradigm shift in this study. He is working with the vocabulary of the "missional church," a theological discourse that in the last several decades has taken seriously the secularization of formerly Christian western Christendom and the reclamation of the fundamental missionary calling of the church. His theological assumptions echo David Bosch's interpretation of our present day reality as "paradigm shift in mission theology." But this shift is to be engaged as the challenge not to reject but to "transform mission" which will mean that we are to be "transformed by mission." This is the thrust of Bosch's magisterial work, *Transforming Mission: Paradigm Shift in Mission Theology* (Maryknoll, NY: Orbis, 2011). This means that we learn to do our theologies of the Christian mission as an alternative paradigm to what our cultural context seeks to impose upon us. The easy compromises and dilutions of centuries of churchly cooperation with culture are now replaced by the hard and challenging task of faithful witness in cultures whose dominant paradigms want to render that witness voiceless.

As the missional theological project continues to expand and deepen, it becomes rapidly clear that an essential aspect of this exploration is precisely the question: How do we relate, as post-Christendom Christian witnesses, to the centuries of Christendom that precede us? It's an enormously important question, because we are still profoundly shaped by that legacy. Christendom still flavors the water in which we swim. The idea that there is such a thing as a "Christian state" or "society" still spooks around in our heads. It should not surprise us that there are still well-meaning attempts to put prayer back in schools, the Ten Commandments on the walls of courthouses, and "Christ back into Christmas."

By proposing that we encounter St. Patrick as a mentor of Christian witness in the realities of fifth-century Ireland, Lockhart challenges one of the most tempting distortions to enter into our grappling with the end of Christendom. It is very easy, from the perspective of post-Christendom paradigms, to assume that God has been absent from this long and complicated history we call Christendom. It's as though we were to agree that the Holy Spirit left Western history somewhere around 100 A.D. and just returned with the emergence of our particular group or sect. Such a reading of the story makes it possible to dismiss Christendom as a misbegotten distortion of Christianity. And there is plenty in that history to support such a judgment. We inherit from Christendom a myriad of reductionisms, distortions, and cultural captivities of the gospel for which we are held accountable. We dare not try to avoid dealing with that confused history. However, to dismiss the entire history of Western Christendom as irrelevant to us today is ultimately an heretical approach. It is questioning the promised presence of God in out world and history. It is denying that Jesus meant it when he said, "Lo, I am with you always, to the close of the Age" (Matt 28:20). It is fail to see that the gospel message was, in fact, proclaimed, heard, responded to, and obeyed in one cultural context after another and in response to constant challenges. We are Christians today because the monks of Christendom faithfully copied out that written legacy over the centuries, and missionaries like Patrick claimed the biblical vision of mission and allowed it to shape them and their actions in Ireland and beyond.

What we need to learn to do is to read our Christendom history dialectically. It is a very human story with ample evidence of our frailty and rebellion. But it is also God's story interacting inextricably with our own, God's faithfulness asserting itself in spite of our rebellion, God's kindness revealing itself when we deserved only pity and punishment. Throughout the intervening centuries, we benefit from the testimony of remarkable Christian witnesses who are truly serving as "Christ's letter to the world" (2 Cor 3:2–3). We don't encounter this "cloud of witnesses" in spiritual isolation from human weakness and sinfulness, but constantly interacting with it. The great saints of the church are all forgiven sinners, but as such, they are often wonderful instruments of God's healing work and God's hopeful promises at work in our communities.

This is, I think, one of the chief theological gifts of Ross Lockhart's work: his exposition of Patrick's life and ministry serves us as a guide for how to deal with the contradictions and tensions of Christendom. We read these accounts both gratefully and warily, sensitive to God's presence at work and equally sensitive to human dilutions of the divine word. As we learn to do that, we make wonderful discoveries: liturgical resources of great beauty and profound spirit, practices of neighborliness that teach us faithful witness, artistic representations of gospel truths in the work of Irish sculptors and architects. It is no wonder that there has been in the last decades a major rediscovery of Celtic spirituality. At its best these practices are truly concrete examples of the "equipping of the saints for the work of service" (Eph 4:10).

The human-divine chemistry of the Irish paradigm of mission includes the admixture of the historically reliable and the hagiographical. It is a delicate task to read and receive appreciatively and yet also critically. That is always the challenge when we are seeking to come to terms with the Christendom legacy and its particular problems for us who now live after Christendom. There is much that we would like to know about Patrick and his companions that the sources do not tell us. And there is a great deal of human imagination that has worked creatively to fill in some of those historical gaps. It is more appropriate preparation for faithful witness to learn here, as well, to read and receive the stories dialectically. The human and the divine are woven together, and we cannot ultimately separate them any more than we should disentangle the roots of the weeds from those of the good wheat in Jesus' parable (Matt 13:24–30).

As the reader will learn from this book, Patrick's spiritual journey begins in the Christendom of his day, and in many ways, his conversion to his apostolic vocation comes together with his insight into the problems of that Christendom. Thus, his missionary witness in Ireland is coupled with a vision and practice of Christian community that is one of the great missional gifts for all times. He is genuinely a renewer of the Christian church. So, Patrick's mission is not adequately summarized by references to snakes and shamrocks. It is about discovery leading to conversion, and out of conversion to the practice of Christian witness that results in the expansion of the Christian mission across Ireland and over to Scotland and ultimately northern Europe. On the remote fringes of fifth-century Europe, God's Spirit claims a man and shapes him through a difficult life story to serve as a witness and an equipper of witnesses to the gospel of God's redeeming love in Jesus Christ. And at the heart of this missional pilgrimage we find remarkable examples of the revival of the ancient apostolic mission, now in forms that relate sensitively and obediently to the world into which God sent Patrick and his company.

The history of western Christendom has many stories like this that merit our attention. As the paradigm shift from western Christendom to post-Christian secularism continues, we need to rediscover these remarkable chapters of missional faithfulness, not just out of historical interest, but as crucial resources for our own equipping to be, do, and say faithful witness to the good news of Jesus Christ's reign.

Preface

Patrick's Moonlit Blessing

The names of a land show the heart of the race;
they move on the tongue like the lilt of a song. . . .
Even suppose that each name were freed from legend's ivy
and history's moss, there'd be music still in, say, Carrick-a-rede.

—John Hewitt, Ulster Names

For hundreds of years my ancestors have farmed the same plot of land, in the rolling green hills in the north of Ireland. My roots are intimately tied up with generations of kinfolk who defined their lives by six day a week farming, good wholesome "craic" on Saturday nights, and Sunday Sabbath keeping as only stoic Presbyterians know how. Whenever I return home to our family farm, I am always amazed by the powerful and enduring witness of this deep pastoral practice—the country rhythm, the ebb and flow of rural life marked by cow milking, sheep tending, God honoring and neighbor-caring relationships.

Down the road from the Lockhart family farm sits the wee town of Markethill. From the steps of our Presbyterian church, you hear the muffled sound of cars whizzing by on the A28, heading north past Gosford Park and through a verdant landscape dotted with bleating sheep, only minutes away from the heart of the ecclesiastical capital of all Ireland—Armagh. Visitors to this "off-the-beaten-path" city first catch a glimpse of the community through the sight of church spires rising in the distance that mark the location of two massive cathedrals that each bear the same name—one

Protestant and the other Catholic. Both places of worship are named after Patricius, the kidnapped shepherd turned missionary disciple, known
today as St. Patrick. The story of this first Bishop of Armagh in 444 AD,
with its truth located somewhere between history and hagiography, is well
known around the world, including his famous object lesson for the Trinity—the three leaf clover. Now, whether Patrick ever actually used plant life
to try and explain the Triune God to ordinary people is doubtful. Rather, it
leaves one to ponder what metaphor Patrick, the great missionary to a pre-
Christian people, would have us reach for in our post-Christendom context today. What many of us can agree on, however, is that we could most
certainly use his help. For today in North America from congregations to
coffee shops, presbyteries to playgrounds, seminaries to supper tables there
is a need for St. Patrick's confident witness in "firmly confessing Threeness
of Persons, Oneness of Godhead, Trinity blest."

In the Pacific Northwest of North America in particular, the unravel-
ing of Christendom has become evident throughout the region known as
Cascadia. Census data on both sides of the border is clear that "no religion"
is now the number one religion in the region.[1] Tina Block's historical sur-
vey of faith in Cascadia found that "Northwest secularity is most evident
in the region's strikingly low levels of involvement in, and attachment to,
formal or organized religion."[2] Some believe that the quick pace of that un-
raveling in Oregon, Washington State, and British Columbia is due, in part,
to the reality that Christendom was never fully established here compared
to back east.[3] Whatever the reason, Cascadia is proving to be fertile ground

1. Block, *The Secular Northwest*, 2. In her scholarly treatment of religion in Cascadia, Block argues that historically "Northwesterners were part of a regional culture that
placed relatively little importance on formal religious connections."

2. Block, *The Secular Northwest*, 48.

3. Matthew Kaemingk identified some of those distinctive marks at the 2016 Fuller
Northwest *Christ and Cascadia* conference in Seattle: 1. A high value on creation. 2. High
mobility of residents with few born in the region 3. A rugged individualism marked by
Cascadians' social isolation. 4. A broad experience of "spirituality" with a hesitation to
place that spirituality within organized religion. 5. Innovation and industry define the
vocational aspirations of Cascadians (e.g., headquarters of Microsoft, Amazon, Costco,
Expedia, Lululemon). 6. Globalization—Cascadia that once thrived on raw materials but
now is fully integrated into the world's economy and social networks. 7. Justice—there
is a commonly held value for social justice and fairness amongst Cascadians. 8. Respect
for and appreciation of Indigenous Communities is common throughout the region.
9. Beauty—both in nature and what human beings create is a commonly held value.
10. Wholeness and emptiness—the wealth, power, and comfort of many Cascadians
gives them a sense of false wholeness. They don't see themselves as people in need of

for sowing seeds of missional leadership that takes seriously Lesslie Newbigin's vision that the West has become the new mission field. Newbigin declared that today Christians are forced to do something that we have not had to do since the birth of the church, namely to discover the "form and substance of a missionary church in terms that are valid in a world that has rejected the power and influence of the Western nations. Missions will no longer work along the stream of expanding Western power. They have to learn to go against the stream."[4]

For over 1,500 years Christianity enjoyed a privileged place in Western society. From Emperor Constantine's embrace (or perhaps we might say domestication) of the Christian Church in the fourth century A.D., followers of Jesus have lived within a larger culture that granted Christianity and its leaders access to power and a seat at the mainstream cultural table. Describing the reality of Christendom, Missiologist Stephan Paas suggests that the average person in the West:

> would be baptized as a child, and he or she would grow up in a society where everything expressed and confirmed religious belief. A certain number of these Christians would be active in their local parish, study the Scriptures, and maintain a life of prayer and good works. Many others would be fairly inactive, but they would be counted as Christians nonetheless.[5]

In a recent conversation with Stephan Paas at Princeton Theological Seminary, he suggested to me that a helpful way of understanding Christendom identity is to think in terms of how people view democracy in the West today. For example, even though not everyone eligible to vote turns out to cast a ballot, some in society would struggle to name the major politicians of the day, and even fewer citizens hold formal membership in a political party, yet the majority would absolutely endorse democracy as a necessary worldview. In a similar way, Christendom Christianity may not have required an active knowledge of, or participation in Christian belief and practice, but there was still a nominal sense of connection with Christian identity.

For many in our churches, they can still remember a time growing up in Canada or the United States where this Christendom reality was

---

community, help, purpose, direction, or salvation. These are things the church normally offers.

4. Newbigin, *The Open Secret*, 5.

5. Paas, *Church Planting in the Secular West*, 90.

commonplace. In the twentieth century, however, secularization began to move throughout the Western world, slowly eroding the church's privileged place in society. What does this look like? Canadian scholar Charles Taylor observes that in the West, "the shift to secularity . . . consists . . . of a move from a society where belief in God is unchallenged and indeed, unproblematic, to one in which it is understood to be one option among others, and frequently not the easiest to embrace."[6] Today, one of the most rapidly growing segments of the North American population is people with little to no knowledge of Christian teachings or practice.[7] What might this look like in a typical community across the West?

> Very secularized nations are characterized by low and decreasing levels of church attendance, low and decreasing levels of other types of church involvement (baptism, church weddings, Christian funerals, etc) widespread lack of belief in traditional Christian doctrines (a personal God, the divinity of Jesus Christ, heaven and hell, etc.), a general indifference towards traditional religious questions (apatheism) and cultural elites that are often quite critical of religion and religious institutions.[8]

Therefore, if we are no longer in the era of Western Christendom then surely our ministerial leadership of Christian witnessing communities must look, feel, and sound different from when we were in that period of privilege ushered in by Constantine. While some may look at the end of Christendom with despair, many of us see an incredible opportunity to shape and share Christian witness free from the limitations of a reduced gospel that our cultural captivity demanded. It is also important to not slip into the deist critique of Christendom that offers the impression that God was absent from the world and church for fifteen hundred years. One way to joyfully minister in the ruins of Christendom is to look for examples of missional leadership in a time and place where Christendom was not yet established. By missional, I mean that the essential vocation of the church is to be God's called and sent people in the world, trusting that rather than the church having a mission, God's mission has a church.[9] This mission

6. Taylor, *A Secular Age*, 3.

7. Paulsen, *Christian Foundations*, 8.

8. Paas, *Church Planting*, 4–5.

9. Guder, ed., *Missional Church*, 11. Rooted in a deep witness to the Triune God, Guder defines missional ecclesiology as biblical, historical, contextual, eschatological and possible for all disciples to practice.

includes the eschatological vision of the healing of the nations and invites us in this time and place to live into the promise that "God was reconciling the world to himself in Christ, not counting people's sins against them. And he has committed to us the message of reconciliation."[10] Therefore, with a deep trust to the witness of the Triune God, missional leadership recognizes that God's being and doing are one, and since God's actions always flow from who God is as Father, Son, and Holy Spirit, so too should the church seek to unify its being and doing.[11] Patrick's movement from being a cultural Christian to a slave in a pre-Christian context, conversion by the Triune God and courageous return to minister with faithful Christian witness in the very place of captivity, offers vivid and essential lessons for our missional leadership today in North America.[12]

As we explore the story of this shepherd slave turned shepherd of souls, there is power still in the legacy of Patrick, when yoked with the Spirit-filled presence and purpose of the risen Christ. Patrick's blessing is waiting to fall on a new mission field where ministering in the name of Jesus can feel like a journey to Hibernia—the ends of the earth. As Northern Irish poet John Hewitt once remarked in his work *Ulster Names*:

> You say Armagh, and I see the hill
> With the two tall spires or the square low tower;
> The faith of Patrick is with us still;
> His blessing falls in a moonlight hour,
> When the apple orchards are all in flower.

---

10. 2 Corinthians 5: 19, NIV.

11. Sparks, Soerens, and Friesen, *The New Parish*, 81. As the Parish Collective argue, "Mission cannot be conceived as a project of the church, rather, the church exists within God's reconciling mission."

12. The language of "pre-Christian" can be problematic for some. Using the language of Pagan often doesn't help matters either. By using "pre-Christian" I am not trying to reinforce triumphalist (and naïve) understandings of conversion through imperial might as was so often the case throughout Christendom. Rather, I am seeking a term to describe a culture that has not been rigorously engaged by Christian witness.

Acknowledgements

*"I am greatly in debt to God. He gave me
such great grace . . . "*

—St. Patrick, *Confession*

THE FARMER WAVED GOOD morning across the backyard fence, his
Wellies sinking deep into the thick mud of the Irish countryside as he
stepped down from his tractor. The rain was lashing the driveway as I
exited the back door of the manse and greeted my neighbor warmly, saying, "Morning! What a terrible day. Can you believe this rain?" The man
smiled and shook his head slowly sideways as raindrops danced on the
top of his tweed cap. "Och aye, Reverend," came the reply in a thick Ulster
accent, "but you must remember that any day the Lord makes *is a great
day!*" I smiled at his gentle, pastoral rebuke and agreed that it *was* best
to give God thanks for everything around us, including the rain. "You're
right, today *is* a great day." And as I smiled at the farmer through the Irish
mist, I could see clearly again the lasting effects from St. Patrick's evangelization of Ireland that continues to bear fruit in people to this day. It was
a helpful and necessary lesson in grace and gratitude.

Writing this book has been another lesson in grace and gratitude due,
in large part, to the encouragement I've received along the way from family
and friends. I am thankful for great colleagues at St. Andrew's Hall and the
other colleges at the University of British Columbia where I am privileged
to teach, including the Vancouver School of Theology, Regent College, and
St. Mark's College. Specifically I want to thank Richard Topping, Robert

Paul, Stephen Farris, Jason Byassee, Darrell Guder, and Jonathan Wilson for their good humor and kindly support.

I am thankful for my home congregation of St. Andrew's/St. Stephen's Presbyterian Church in North Vancouver where I serve as Minister-in-Association with my friend and pastor Martin Baxter. Martin's passion for the gospel and exceedingly dry Irish humor are a source of great blessing and inspiration for my own ministry.

I am also grateful for the friendships I have developed in the Presbyterian Church in Ireland (PCI) while visiting the Lockhart family in Ulster over the years. I especially want to acknowledge the PCI congregations and clergy that graciously welcomed me into their pulpits on exchange, including Markethill, Tullyallen, Mount Norris, and Free Duff Presbyterian churches in Armagh; Kirkpatrick Memorial and Fitzroy Presbyterian Churches in Belfast, Ballywillan Presbyterian Church in Port Rush and Wexford and Enniscorthy Presbyterian Churches in the South as well as St. Patrick's Church of Ireland Cathedral, Armagh. The people of these congregations taught me much about grace and gratitude that is at the heart of the gospel of Jesus Christ, and I hope those lessons have found its way into what you read here.

I am appreciative for the opportunity to draw on the resources of many theological libraries close to home in Vancouver but in particular I wish to acknowledge the collection at Union Theological College, Belfast, the University of Toronto and Princeton Theological Seminary in New Jersey that aided me in this work. Sharing my research and writing in various stages of development with others was helpful including speaking at Fuller Seminary Northwest's *Christ and Cascadia* conference in Seattle, St. Peter's Fireside church plant in Vancouver, the Parish Collective's Inhabit Conference in Seattle (theological educator's panel), the Revitalize Conference at Metropolitan Church, London, the Presbyterian Synod of Manitoba and Northwestern Ontario, as well as the Renewal Conference for the Presbytery of the Kootenays in scenic Crawford Bay, British Columbia.

It was such a pleasure working again with the good folks at Cascade Books and I appreciate their assistance in bringing this project to completion. I wish to express my heartfelt thanks to the staff for their support and encouragement throughout the publishing process, especially to my editor Rodney Clapp who once again helped to make my work a more faithful witness to the gospel.

Finally, I thank my family for their love and support. My wife Laura is an incredible source of strength, love and encouragement to me as we cheerfully navigate life and ministry together in response to God's call. Together, we delight in raising our children Emily, Jack, and Sadie on the slopes of Grouse Mountain in beautiful North Vancouver. Yes, grace and gratitude seem like a suitable response to the many blessings of my life as I recall the wisdom of that Irish farmer—every day the Lord makes is a great day. Or as St. Patrick said so beautifully in his *Confession,* "This is how we can repay such blessings, when our lives change and we come to know God, to praise and bear witness to his great wonders before every nation under heaven."

Ross A. Lockhart
St. Andrew's Hall, Vancouver

Introduction

Vox Cascadia

"Life is man and place and these have names."

—"Landscape," by John Hewitt

I spent the weekend recently on beautiful Vancouver Island, connecting with Presbyterian colleagues in Victoria and preaching on the Sunday morning. My family stayed in Cook Street Village, a delightful little neighborhood on the other side of Cobble Hill Park from James Bay. It is a trendy, eclectic spot where one finds a curious mix of hipsters and homeless, boutique shops and small cafes, an organic grocery store and an obligatory Starbucks, resting comfortably side by side.

As I strolled through the village with my family, there was one establishment that caught my eye in particular. I stopped and stared as my children stood beside me, slightly confused and momentarily speechless. It wasn't a medical marijuana dispensary or a yoga studio—those are a dime a dozen in Cascadia. No, it was something old school called "Pic-A-Flic." The children finally broke the silence, pointing at movement coming in and out of the business, saying, "Dad, what are those people doing?" I blinked and stammered, "Well, um, they appear to be going into a store where I think they are paying money to rent movies." Silence. I continued, "You see, they have to physically take those DVDs home, watch them and then eventually return them to this store." More silence. One of the children then queried, "So, like, they have to bring the video back in person?" I nodded silently without taking my eyes off the sight. My son continued, "So, they actually have to *get in their car*, drive back to this location *and* hand in the video?" "Yes, that's it," I said, snapping back to life and getting a bit more excited now, "and guess what? If they are late returning the video they have to *pay extra money in fines*. Imagine that!" Further silence. Wheels turning. "Um, Dad, why don't these people just get Netflix or something?" the children asked innocently. "I don't know," I replied with a mix of astonishment and curiosity. And then the words just slipped out of my mouth, "I didn't realize that people *did that kind of thing anymore*."

Instantly, I realized that I had heard those same words before in Vancouver, Seattle, and Portland in coffee shops talking to strangers or chatting with parents on the soccer pitch or at swimming lessons. "Where do you work?" comes the question. "Oh, the church . . . I'm a pastor." Silence. And then the inevitable reply, "Really, I didn't realize that *people do that anymore?*" Welcome to Cascadia.

Irish poet John Hewitt offers up a thesis in his work *Landscapes*, where he argues that life is about people (women and men and children) and places (home and work and play) and their specific names help give shape, clarity, and meaning to the world around us. Names, for example, like Cascadia or Hibernia. These are names of places that also give shape and meaning to the people who live there. While at first glance a book that tries to draw lessons for twenty-first century Cascadia from fifth-century Hibernia may feel like a bit of a stretch, but the more I have explored the witness of the church at the margins of empire in St. Patrick's ministry, the more missional treasure I have found for us today in the West.

Indeed, somewhere in the mists of time between history and hagiography stands the great evangelist and missionary St. Patrick. Raised a "cultural Christian," Patrick's encounter with the Triune God during captivity in Ireland transformed his life and the history of a people. Freedom from slavery, and a return home to Britain, produced the divine summons—*Vox Hibernia*—to return to Ireland and the place of captivity in order to witness to the gospel of Jesus Christ. Christian witness in twenty-first century Vancouver, Seattle or Portland is a world away from fifth-century Armagh, Slane, or Cashel. Yet, the great evangelist to pre-Christian peoples of Hibernia has much to teach us as we seek to engage our secular, post-Christian context. There is wisdom in the missional leadership of the one we call St. Patrick that goes well beyond tales of snakes and shamrocks. This book is a response to the questions that I've wrestled with for some time now as a pastor and a professor: "What lessons might Patrick hold for us in the

Pacific Northwest specifically, and the broader Western culture in general, as we seek to witness to the gospel in a post-Christendom culture? How might the missiological experience with pre-Christian peoples direct our contemporary missiological encounter with post-Christian peoples? What might God's call to us mean if we were to respond to *Vox Cascadia*?"

More than half a century ago, C. S. Lewis warned in a letter written on St. Patrick's Day that witnessing to post-Christian peoples can be even more difficult than the kind of pre-Christian that Patrick encountered in Ireland. Lewis wrote, "They err who say: 'The world is turning pagan again.' Would that it were! The truth is, we are falling into a much worse state. Post-Christian man is not the same as pre-Christian man. He is as far removed as a virgin from a widow."[1] Mindful of this challenge, we approach this work with a deep trust in the reality of the *Missio Dei* that shaped witnessing communities of Christians in the past and continues to do so today in our time and place. As my colleague Mark Glanville reminds us from the perspective of the whole biblical story, "Mission is the encounter with the world of a community gathered by Christ to be caught up in the Father's reconciling purpose for all of his creation, living by the Spirit as a sign, instrument and foretaste of Christ's restorative reign."[2] Therefore, we pay (or perhaps pray?) attention to the ancient/future context contrast between Hibernia and Cascadia as a way of discerning the ongoing patterns of God's missional engagement with the world. As Michael Goheen reminds us, "Mission has its source in the love of the Father who sent his Son to reconcile all things to himself. The Son sent the Spirit to gather his church together and empower it to participate in this mission. This church is sent by Jesus to continue his mission, and this sending defines its very nature."[3]

Taking the Irish poet John Hewitt at his word, life is about our humanity, the places we inhabit and the names we ascribe to them. Therefore, I have structured *Vox Cascadia* as a journey between the ancient-future places of Patrick's Ireland and our Pacific Northwest today. Each chapter reflects a different geographic place, its name representing the old evangelist's encounter

---

1. Lewis, "Letter to Don Giovanni Calabria, March 17, 1953," *Collected Letters, Volume 2*. More recently George Lindbeck and Stanley Hauerwas have picked up on this argument in postliberal theology.

2. Glanville, "A Missional Reading of Deuteronomy," in *Reading the Bible Missionally*, Goheen, ed., 125.

3. Goheen, ed., *Reading the Bible Missionally*, 8. As Goheen argues, "Mission is not merely a set of outreach activities: *it defines the very being of God's people*."

with a pre-Christian people as he went about witnessing to the power of the gospel in the person and work of Jesus Christ, crucified and risen.

The journey begins in Chapter One that is centered on Bannaventa Berniae, a reflection on Patrick's upbringing in Roman Britain complete with lukewarm "cultural Christianity." Thanks to his nominally Christian parents and a faith that did not take root in young Patricius, he was well on his way to being a member of the church's alumni association by his teenage years. This chapter is an invitation for us to reflect on the legacy of the Christendom experiment in North America that has (thankfully) come to an end. Yet sadly, this legacy has too often produced malnourished disciples and anemic apostles who cannot discern between the flavor of true gospel saltiness and the bland stew of popular culture. Through the lens of Exile, we explore the shift in the mainline church in North America where today there is both awareness of, and despair for, the decline of the church over the last fifty years. It is possible to see the death of cultural Christianity as a blessing, however, as we recognize that cultures and communities washed in the gospel but not responsive to sanctification by the Holy Spirit will surely "wither and die."[4]

Patrick's story shifts us in Chapter Two, in a rather dramatic fashion, to a strikingly different place and people. From western Britain we travel to the bleak hillside of Slemish in the north of Ireland, where Patrick was kept as a slave and shepherd. Here, the Triune God revealed himself to the kidnapped and captive Patrick in a powerful and transformative way. Slemish stands as a place of revelation. In the post-Christendom West, we are in desperate need of that same transformative revelation of the Father, Son, and Holy Spirit. This deep and prayerful attentiveness to the calling of God on our lives must be matched by an urgent sense of obedience to play our part in God's unfolding drama of reconciliation and redemption in the world. Our desire for revival is matched by our acknowledgment that it only happens by God's action and in God's own timing.

Chapter Three moves us back across the Irish Sea from slavery to freedom, like the Israelites crossing the Red Sea with Egyptian chariots in pursuit. Patrick's dramatic, divinely inspired escape from Hibernia leads him back to an emotional reunion with family and friends. This chapter

---

4. In the Presbyterian Church of Canada's *Living Faith/Foi Vivante* there is this crucial reminder: "Baptism is also an act of discipleship that requires commitment and looks towards growth in Christ. Those baptized in infancy are called in later years to make personal profession of Christ. What is born may die. What is grafted may wither. Congregations and those baptized must strive to nurture life in Christ." (7.6.4)

is entitled "Uillula," the Latin word for family estate, and reflects Patrick's return home to Roman Britain with its sense of order and civilization. Patrick returns a changed man, however, and his homecoming also produces feelings of restlessness. It is here that he receives the divine summons, "Vox Hibernia," the voice or call of the Irish to return to his former place of captivity to share the gospel. How do we hear God's voice and understand our vocation as disciples in a post-Christendom reality today? How might the Triune God be summoning us from a place of comfort and quietness to risk a daring missional engagement with the world?

Ironically, Chapter Four moves us further away from Ireland in order to fulfill Patrick's calling to Hibernia. To complete his theological studies, it is believed that Patrick moved to Auxerre, France. Patrick, in a Magi-like move, goes "home by another road" and is prepared for his future church work by a theological education model more conditioned to producing parish priests than missionaries to foreign lands. This leads us to reflect on our own methods of theological education in North America today, and the Pacific Northwest in particular, as we struggle to prepare future leaders no longer for caretaking ministries in well-established, thriving Christendom congregations but rather missional and entrepreneurial leadership for new and renewed witnessing communities in a culture that is hostile to the gospel.

Chapter Five takes us with Patrick and his companions to the shores of Hibernia and his first church plant at Saul. While not the first Christian missionary to Ireland (that honor belongs to Palladius), Patrick takes the next most faithful step in response to Vox Hibernia. His church planting efforts in Ireland were daring and dangerous. His risk for the gospel would end up glorifying God and enhancing Christ's reputation to the ends of the earth. At the edge of North America, Cascadia is home today to a growing number of church plants as Christians experiment in planting and replanting dinner churches and house church movements. How might God be at work establishing new "Saul-like" communities of small Christian witness on the rocky shores of the secular Northwest and beyond?

Not long into Patrick's ministry he came into conflict with the existing culture and spiritual values present and preserved by the people. Chapter Six explores the reality of resistance to the gospel preached and lived in society. For Patrick, a memorable encounter with "powers and principalities" came on the eve of Easter when he found himself on the hill of Slane, lighting a paschal flame to signal the light of Christ bursting forth from the grave at

Easter. This act of daring witness during the Easter vigil led him onto a collision course with the local Druid priests and the High King of Tara. Christian witness in a post-Christendom culture also brings Christ-followers into conflict with dominant culture values and the secular priests of our day. How might we find the courage and Christ-like clarity to name the idols present in our culture, the reality of sin around and within us, and move people to a confession of faith in the God we know in Jesus?

Of course, while there is resistance to the gospel preached, the good news of God's saving action in Christ also moves many to a state of repentance and conversion to the mission of Jesus. Despite the hostility of some in Hibernia, Patrick's ministry also awakened a great many to a life of faith in Christ. Cashel stands as a powerful example of this. In Chapter Seven, we explore Patrick's ministry at Cashel that led the king of Munster to repentance of sin and baptism into a new life with Christ. With the end of Christendom, fewer and fewer people are baptized as infants out of social conditioning. As a result, many Christian communities are experiencing a growing number of adult converts to the faith. For mainline churches in particular, this presents a fascinating change in how people enter into the church. How might we harness this new work of the Holy Spirit for the building up of the body of Christ in the post-Christendom West?

As Patrick's ministry flourished in Ireland, there was a need to develop a structure and more robust ecclesiology. Patrick made the decision to center his ministry in the north of Ireland, in the community that we call Armagh today. In Chapter Eight, we watch Patrick shape the church in Ireland into something that would outlast his ministry and affect the children of God in Hibernia long after he passed into the communion of saints. Today in the West, denominational structures developed during Christendom are failing. Denominational headquarters in Christendom often mirrored corporate headquarters with large physical plants, division of labor into various departments and operations flowcharts more suited to building cars than nurturing communities of gospel witness. With the decline of the formerly mainline denominations, there is an opportunity for us to ask questions of ecclesiology and mission afresh so that we may be most faithful in this generation as the church engages the world for the sake of the gospel.

In Chapter Nine, we explore a particular form of ecclesiastical community used by Patrick and his followers in Ireland that continues to develop in today's post-Christendom church. Monasterboice serves as an example of a monastic community that developed in the wake of Patrick's ministry. Monasticism's countercultural Christian witness and shared common life in a particular place, has helped inspire Christians in North America through the New Monasticism movement. These intentional Christian communities are strong in the Pacific Northwest as well, where young Christians are seeking to live a 24/7 commitment to the gospel in relationship with others in a particular neighborhood.

Following Jesus in the world leads one into conflict with sin on a personal and corporate level. As a follower of Jesus, Patrick felt compelled to speak up and speak out against injustice, proclaiming God's truth to power, no matter what the cost. In Chapter Ten, we examine "Letter to the soldiers of Coroticus," which is one of only two written documents that survived Patrick's ministry. In it we read of his righteous anger at the slave trading of a "so-called" Christian from Roman Britain, enslaving people in Ireland in a ironic reversal of what Patrick experienced as a teenage boy. In the letter, Patrick calls out the leaders of the slave trade after newly baptized Christians under his care are attacked and hauled off to captivity from a place called Ail. In Christendom, the church had both access to political power and was often domesticated by it. Instead of "plundering the Egyptians," the church more often was "plundered by the Egyptians," propping up unjust regimes or participating in activities that brought dishonor to Christ.[5] In Canada, for example, the church's participation in Residential Schools led representatives of Christ in cooperation with the government to seize Indigenous children from their homes and strip them of their culture in order to westernize First Nations. This unholy action of racial discrimination and cultural destruction was often accompanied by horrifying acts of physical and sexual abuse. As Christians now living in a post-Christendom culture, how might we work for justice in a way that brings glory to God without access to traditional forms of temporal power?

In Chapter Eleven we explore the Christian practice of pilgrimage. Patrick's life and ministry has inspired countless Christians over the centuries to participate in pilgrimage as a way of connecting with God and deepening their relationship with Christ. Croagh Patrick in County Mayo is one of those sites of pilgrimage. A holy mountain, pilgrims even walk barefoot up the rocky slopes remembering Patrick's time there and communing with the Trinity! Pilgrimage is a strong image for this Christian

---

5. A favorite reversal of Augustine's advice from *On Doctrine* used by my colleague Richard Topping.

journey in the post-Christendom West. We are journeying into territory that is unfamiliar and yet holds the promise of God's revelation at every turn. How might we yoke pilgrimage and witness to the Triune God in the places where we live, work and play? What might it mean to discover Jesus anew as our "holy site?"

Our journey ends at Downpatrick, the traditional place of Patrick's burial. Chapter Twelve explores the legacy of the saint to Hibernia as his story now literally reaches the ends of the earth. What lessons might we take away from Patrick's life and ministry that could impact our practice and witness for Christ today? As resurrection people we acknowledge that by grace, even what appears to be an end can be a new beginning. As we contemplate the end of church as we have known it in Western Christendom, what story will be told years from now when people pause and look back on the work and witness of the church in this generation of believers? Where might we point today to evidence of the Holy Spirit at work around us, bringing forth new life as a foretaste of the heavenly banquet to come?

This journey between the landscapes of Hibernia and Cascadia offers us the opportunity to compare, contrast, and contemplate what faithful Christian witness might look like in a world where the frontier of mission sits at the doorstep of every home, at the edge of every work desk, at the corner of every barista bar and the sidelines of every sports field. The landscape between Hibernia and Cascadia may look very different at first glance, but upon closer inspection we see the same dynamic, divine dance of the Father, Son, and Holy Spirit drawing sinful and broken humanity into a relationship that is reconciled and made new. As John Hewitt once said, "the living landscape is a map of kinship . . . landscape is families . . . and life is man and place and these have names."[6]

6. In Longley and Ormsby, eds., *The Selected Poems of John Hewitt*, 56–65.

CHAPTER ONE

Bannaventa Berniae

Growing Up Christian

It will be people with a passionate conviction of God's power to transform our present situation who will evangelize today.

—ALAN J. ROXBURGH, *REACHING A NEW GENERATION*

ST. PATRICK WAS BORN in Roman Britain around 387 AD[1] at Bannaventa Berniae,[2] a settlement difficult to pinpoint on a map but believed to be somewhere on the west coast of Britain, possibly in Cumbria.[3] St. Patrick, or Patricius as he was known then, was a preacher's kid.[4] His grandfather Potitus was a priest and his father Calpornius was a deacon and town

---

1. Like most things with Patrick, there are a variety of opinions regarding the date of his birth and ministry in Ireland. While tradition suggests Patrick was born around 390 AD with his mission in Ireland between 432 AD and 461, some scholars have suggested Patrick was actually born later closer to 415 with ministry in Ireland between 461 to 493 AD.

2. There are many different spellings of Patrick's hometown including "Bannauem Taburniae" and simply "Taburnia," meaning "the field of the tents," in reference to a place where Roman Legions once pitched their tents.

3. There are, of course, wide-ranging opinions as well on where exactly Patrick was born and raised on the west coast of what we now call Wales, England, and Scotland. Out of an enduring love for St. Patrick, as well as a good dose of nationalistic pride, the question of whether Patrick was Welsh, English, or Scottish can still create a little controversy. What is most important for our reflections, however, is simply to note that he was a Roman Briton, raised within an empire on the decline.

4. Patrick's full Latin name according to tradition was "Magonus Sucatus Patricius."

councilor.[5] There is no evidence, however, that Patrick came from a family of great evangelical conviction and it is far more likely that his Dad took on the role less out of pietistic commitment and more out of practicality, as the position came with great financial advantages.[6] Patrick lived a comfortable life. As Jonathan Rogers notes, "He was a good Roman—a Latin-speaking son of Roman wealth and Roman privilege. . . . Patrick's Roman *bona fides* were impeccable. His given name was the Latin Patricius, which means 'highborn,' and indeed he was."[7] Patrick's home would have been comfortable: "the principal rooms of the Romano-British villa were colorfully decorated, and the wall-paintings on plaster generally executed in red, olive-green and brown. Sometimes the ceiling was painted too."[8] While Patrick's family did not belong to the highest order of Roman British society known as "colonia," their status in the lesser administrative unit of "victus" still granted them considerable privilege above the "pagus" or rural folk.[9]

Patrick grew up on the edge of empire but in one of the first generations of Christendom—the fifteen hundred-year experiment of privilege for the Christian church in Western culture. The rise of Christianity in 33 AD nearly coincided with the arrival of the Romans in Britain under Emperor Claudius in 43 AD. Christianity spread throughout Britain as a minor sect along with the more dominant Roman pagan cults. The edict of toleration towards Christians in 311 AD by Emperor Galerius (a week before his death) and Constantine's Edict of Milan in 313 AD removed persecution and moved Christianity from a minority (estimated by some to be as high as 10 percent of the population in the Roman Empire) to a nominal majority by the time of Patrick's birth. How different Patrick's experience of the church would have been growing up than someone in Britain 200 years or more before him. By the late fourth Century, the church in Britain appeared

---

5. Tradition later ascribes the name Concessa as Patrick's mother and wife of Calpornius.

6. One of the roles of the town councilor or "decurion" was being on the hook to collect taxes from locals and having to make up the difference out of one's own pocket if there was a shortfall. Emperor Constantine created a loophole where decurions who were also members of the clergy were exempt from that laborious task and potential financial burden.

7. Rogers, *St Patrick*, 5.

8. De Breffny, *In the Steps of St. Patrick*, 11.

9. De Breffny, *In the Steps of St. Patrick*, 10.

in similar form to that of the rest of the Roman Empire. As Darrell Guder describes the early stages of the Christendom experiment:

> Building on ancient Roman patterns of provinces and territories, the church divided up its realm into manageable units, presided over by bishops. Their districts or dioceses were in turn divided into parishes, and a church with a steeple and a bell was placed at the center of every parish, often on the main square of the village or town. Everyone lived within hearing range of the bells. The calendar that shaped everyone's life was dominated by the themes of the Christian tradition. It was the church's task to ensure that these religious services would always be available to all its members—which was really the entire population.[10]

Emperor Constantine's moderate policies for Christianity beginning in 313 AD, and continuing support of the Christian faith by the Roman establishment (with notable moments of reversal and persecution) throughout the rest of the fourth century meant that Patricius was born into a very different world than that of the New Testament Roman Empire. The church in Roman Britain would have appeared similar to the rest of Europe by the time of Patrick's birth. According to Thomas O'Loughlin, the established church structure of Patrick's day meant "the density of bishops in other parts of the Empire at the time would equally have applied in Britain and that density meant that every town . . . would have a bishop . . . There may have been a bishop of Bannavem Taburniae,"[11] where Patrick grew up. This new, highly structured and state-influenced ecclesiastical world for Christians in the Roman Empire was home for Patricius, including a family that embraced "cultural Christianity" in an era when the world was becoming more unsettled and dangerous.

Indeed, while Christianity was gaining power during this era, other significant events were also shaping the landscape. The Roman Empire was in trouble, as Germanic Visigoths threatened the "Eternal City," eventually sacking Rome in 410 AD and sending shockwaves through the crumbling empire. As with most institutions in trouble, there was a move to centralize power and protect the core. As a result of this crumbling empire, the Roman navy was called home from the Irish Sea to the Mediterranean Sea. This foreign policy move in Rome, however, would have a direct bearing on the future saint of Ireland. With the Roman navy withdrawn, Saxons,

---

10. Guder, "A Missiological Context," unpublished, 8.

11. O'Loughlin, *Discovering Saint Patrick*, 48.

Picts, and Irish sporadically began raiding Roman communities. "Homeland security" took on a new emphasis, as Britons felt threatened in ways they had not experienced since Emperor Claudius arrived ushering in *Pax Romana* with his war elephants and 40,000 Roman soldiers in Britain in 43 AD. One night, when Patricius was sixteen years old and his parents were in the nearby fortified town, Irish raiders attacked their lightly defended villa complex, hauling off slaves, including the young man history now remembers as St. Patrick, beginning his long exile in a foreign land.

Exile is a familiar term for Christians today in North America. The biblical narrative of the people of Israel hauled off into captivity by King Nebuchadnezzar in 586 BC from Jerusalem has been applied to the state of the Euro-stock church in North America for decades. Thanks to scholars like Walter Brueggemann, we are well acquainted in the church today with the language of exile as a way of describing the church in the West. Mark Labberton recently wrote,

> I believe the people of God live in exile. The tantalizing possibilities of getting lost in Promised Land visions live on for many, of course, but others are increasingly realizing it is a mirage. Meanwhile, exile—life as strangers in a strange land—is our context. We have allowed and contributed to a dominant secular culture that has now engulfed us and in which we are ever more fully the minority. We are a declining cultural force against countervailing pressures of spiritual decline. The church of Christendom is fading and flailing.[12]

This fading and flailing means that the church now in exile is recognizing that it is no longer a social or political power-broker but instead has been "chased away from its place of privilege and is now seeking to find where it belongs amid the ever-changing dynamics of contemporary culture."[13]

Nowhere is the end of Christendom and life in exile clearer in North America than here in Cascadia. The kind of leadership now required for missionary disciples is more like the courage and vision of Daniel in the lion's den or the fiery furnace faith of Meshach, Shadrach, and Abednego (or as my real estate agent friend calls them—my shack, your shack and a bungalow). For some of our aging saints in the pews, their lifetime of discipleship has witnessed the church in North American society (as they know it) bundled up and hauled off to a foreign land of despair. This is

12. Labberton, *Called*, 55.

13. Beach, *The Church in Exile*, 46.

4

particularly true for those of us who come from what we might call the "formerly mainline" denominations.

For many, it is forcing us to take a long, hard look at what we've known to be our experience of church and what it means to be disciples of the risen Christ. Missiologist David Fitch suggests that this season of our discipleship in the West is an invitation to rediscover God's faithful presence in the exile-like ruins of Christendom. Today, we are called to witness to the presence of the Triune God in our everyday, ordinary lives. Fitch cautions:

> God's presence is not always obvious. He requires witnesses. God comes humbly in Christ. He so loves us, he never imposes himself on us. Instead he comes to us, to be with us, and in that presence he reveals himself. In his presence there is forgiveness, reconciliation, healing, transformation, patience and, best of all, love. In his presence he renews all things. Presence is how God works. But he requires a people tending to his presence to make his presence visible for all to see.[14]

Australian missional leaders Darren Cronshaw and Kim Hammond concur with Fitch and encourage us to be present to God and neighbor as we live our faithful lives in the world. They suggest, "People look at the pattern of our lives before the proclamation of our words, so they will more likely grasp truth as we live submerged among them, authentically sharing our stories."[15] As we live out the biblical witness in the places were we live, work, and play, we do so with a deep trust that while we may be in exile right now, the God who faithfully shepherded his people Israel through the exodus wilderness always goes ahead of us like a pillar of cloud by day and a pillar of fire by night. Our God of exodus and exile ultimately holds victory in his hands and is moving all things towards reconciliation and the ultimate healing of the nations. As Vancouver missiologist Alan Roxburgh writes, "The biblical narratives are formed in an eschatology—God's movement in, for and with the world toward a future. No organizational system or its leadership can manage, control, encapsulate or program the Spirit's disruptive future."[16]

As a professor, I regularly visit local congregations to meet with church leaders and serve as a guest preacher on Sunday mornings. When visiting these churches, I am curious about discerning God's presence in

14. Fitch, *Faithful Presence*, 27.

15. Cronshaw and Hammond, *Sentness*, 122.

16. Roxburgh, *Structured for Mission*, 103.

the community and how to encourage the followers of Jesus there to bear witness to God's activity amongst them. I sometimes will ask questions like, "Where have you experienced God's grace in this church or community lately?" or "Tell me a story about when you've sensed you're standing on holy ground in this parish" or "If you had to prove the existence of God in this neighborhood, where would you take me?" These questions are an attempt to help people take the next most faithful step towards testimony regarding God's activity in their everyday, ordinary lives. It is an opportunity for them to name God's faithful presence in their lives and find the courage to live into the biblical call to "always be prepared to give to anyone who asks a reason/witness/testimony to the hope that is in you, with gentleness and respect."[17]

The days have thankfully passed when Christendom reduced the gospel to an individualistic "salvation management system" provided by the church, with rites of passage from birth to death to reduce one's chances of hell and increase one's chances of heaven (or at least purgatory in medieval theology).[18] No, in our post-Christendom context, we are called by God to discern his faithful presence in community, no longer being encouraged to be passive by "outsourcing our baptismal vows to paid clergy."[19] Instead, David Fitch suggests we understand our calling to be centered around the "close" (not closed!) circle of the Christian community where Jesus is host and we are guests; our own "dotted circles" of table fellowship in our homes with a mix of believers and non-believers where we serve as host; and "half-circles" in our local neighborhoods (coffee shops, soccer pitches, parent-teacher associations) where we come as guests not to fix or judge but to bear witness to God's faithful presence. Fitch summarizes these three circles that gather, equip and send disciples out into the world by stating, "When God's people become present to God's presence in the world (missio Dei) by making space for Christ's presence to be among them (incarnation), witness happens. In mathematical terms we might put it this way: missio Dei + incarnation = witness. This is faithful presence."[20] Within the

17. 1 Peter 3:15, *NIV*.

18. "Salvation Management System" is a favorite phrase used by Darrell Guder to explain what happens when the Western church reduced the gospel to a manageable and human controllable-sized message.

19. A phrase I often use to describe my pastoral experience of the Christendom legacy at work in local congregations. When people say things like, "Pastor, I don't pray so let's have you do it, isn't that why we pay you?"

20. Fitch, *Faithful Presence*, 202.

pews of our local churches sit the last generation raised in Christendom. As they move through life and face the future, many feel discouraged about the state of the church they know and love. They are worried about what will happen to the buildings and places that they have poured their lives into. St. Patrick was raised in the structured environment of Christendom as well, but found a way to witness in a new and, at times, frightening context. I believe God is still faithfully present in post-Christendom as he was in Christendom. In fact, as Lee Beach argues, contrary to being a disaster, "the exilic experience of losing cultural power and finding ourselves marginalized may indeed be needed to restore the church to its true identity and missional calling."[21] Now, as always, we need God to grant us eyes to see, ears to hear and hearts to love the world as God always has and always will. We need to ask God for the ability to discern his faithful presence in the midst of this new mission field of the West.

I preached recently at a little Presbyterian Church in south Vancouver. As a professor, I am now free on Sundays and spend my Sabbath preaching weekly in local churches of every possible denominational stripe. As I relish this itinerant homiletical gift from God, it is also providing me with fascinating insights as to what the Trinity is up to in different neighborhoods through Cascadia. While I preach in Baptist, Anglican, Brethren, no-name brand community churches, and so forth, the majority of preaching locations are with my own people—God's frozen chosen—the Reformed tribe. When visiting more charismatic churches, I say that you can spot evangelical Presbyterians a mile away—we like to worship God with our hands outside our pockets!

The Sunday I showed up to preach at this local Presbyterian Church, the Clerk of Session greeted me warmly at the door. I met with a couple of elders before worship for prayer and they followed our prayer with a brief history of the congregation. There were once 250 Scottish immigrant families in the neighborhood that filled the church Sunday by Sunday. "We once had to hold Sunday School classes in people's cars parked outside because we had so many children in this church. Things have changed, pastor," the kindly man said with an unmistakable tone of sadness in his voice. I walked with the elders into the beautifully maintained worship space. There were twelve people scattered in the pews before me. It was once again a reminder of the church in exile. As we began to worship the Triune God, however, I noticed that ethnic diversity in that small group

21. Beach, *The Church in Exile*, 230.

of twelve worshippers. People from Korea, China, and the Caribbean were present in worship, and at least one person from Scotland reminding us of Mother Kirk. At the end of the worship service someone announced that they were scheduled for surgery that week and feeling scared. Without hesitation or making a big fuss, the worshippers gathered at the front in a circle, laid on hands, and prayed for the power of the Holy Spirit to descend upon this disciple for courage, strength, and healing in the days to come. In that moment, I was glad to no longer be at home in a Christendom church. I was glad to be taken by the Holy Spirit into exile. I was aware of God's faithful presence in that place.

As I left the worship space that day, I also noted that the church was not just a one-day a week worshipping community for Presbyterians. They also hosted a vibrant English as a Second Language program, after-school activities for neighborhood children, and three other congregations of Korean, Chinese and Spanish Christians met in that space. It is almost as if in exile, we can hear God's voice more clearly, maybe even like hearing it again for the first time. Just like Patrick.

CHAPTER TWO

Slemish

Captivity and Crisis

I was then about sixteen years of age. I did not know the true
God. I was taken into captivity to Ireland with many thousands
of people—and deservedly so, because we turned away from
God, and did not keep His commandments.

—St. Patrick, *Confession*

Hauling him off into exile, the Irish raiders soon sold Patricius to a slave owner, likely somewhere just off Ireland, suggestions include Lambay Island beside Dublin or perhaps Rathlin Island in the north, across from modern Ballycastle and today's Corrymella Community. Who Patrick was sold to and where he spent his captivity is also debated. Some say that he was taken as far west as County Mayo but many suggest it was just north of what we now call Belfast on Slemish Mountain, where he worked for a harsh owner named Milchu. Patrick himself writes, "After I came to Ireland I watched over sheep. Day by day I began to pray more frequently—and more and more my love of God and my faith in him and reverence for him began to increase."[1] This dramatic and unwanted change of social location opened Patrick to the voice of the Triune God in a way that he had never experienced (or perhaps he would even say needed) in his life of affluence

---

1. Patrick, *Confession*, Section 16. In the *Confession* quoted at the beginning of this chapter, you begin to get a sense that Patrick viewed his exile, along with his fellow British slaves, as the consequence of their unfaithfulness to God along the lines of the prophetic warning unheeded in Jeremiah 9:16, "I will scatter them among nations that neither they nor their fathers have known."

9

and comfort back home in Britain. As Phillip Freeman notes, this time as a shepherd slave on an Irish farm was the best preparation for Patrick's future calling as a missionary. Freeman writes:

> Every day he picked up more of the language, so different and yet similar in many ways to his native British. He watched and listened and learned to keep his mouth shut except when he had something important to say. He became familiar with the customs and gods of a foreign land. Not least of all, he learned to look beyond his own immediate desires to care for the needs of his flock. He had to guide them and watch over them, to see that they had enough food to eat and protect them from wolves. It was good practice.[2]

It *was* good practice indeed for his future ministry leadership, just as young ruddy-cheeked David watched over sheep and protected them from enemies long before selecting five smooth stones to face Goliath. As John Calvin notes, "The pastor ought to have two voices: one, for gathering the sheep; and another, for warding off and driving away wolves and thieves. The Scripture supplies him with the means of doing both."[3] Patrick notes the importance of this difficult period in his life for future vocational development: "God used the time to shape and mold me into something better. He made me into what I am now—someone very different from what I once was, someone who can care about others and work to help them. Before I was a slave, I didn't even care about myself."[4]

At Slemish, Patrick had a mountain top moment. The Triune God initiated Patrick's conversion experience with a clear purpose. Jonathan Rogers describes it this way:

> Eugene Peterson speaks of the "God-dominated imagination" that developed in David as he spent his days and nights watching sheep on the Judean hillsides. It appears that something similar happened in Patrick. In the lush, green hills of . . . Ireland, in the towering clouds that rolled across the big sky, even in the most inclement of weather, Patrick sensed the presence of a Creator who hadn't seemed very real or relevant or necessary in his earlier life of ease. For all its disadvantages, the shepherd's life leaves plenty of time to think and pray, and Patrick used his time to great

---

2. Freeman, *St. Patrick of Ireland*, 28–29.

3. Calvin, *Commentaries on the Epistles to Timothy, Titus, and Philemon*, 296.

4. Freeman, *St. Patrick of Ireland*, 184.

advantage. Far from wallowing in self-pity, Patrick celebrated his enslavement, the very shock he needed to bring him to his senses.[5]

Like many of us, Patrick soon discovered in response to God's initiative that we are *saved* to be *sent*. As Karl Barth warns, the purpose of being a Christian is not simply "enjoying the benefits of the gospel" in a consumerist driven model of Christian community.[6] Rather, Barth's teaching reminds us that in gratitude we respond to God's grace and that our primary vocation is to be a witness in the world to God's ongoing mission in the risen Christ to heal the nations. As Barth explains:

> In other words, their calling means both that He reveals Himself in His action and also that He summons them into the witness-box as those who know. As God speaks His Word to these men [sic] in and with what He does, and as He is heard by them, He gives them the freedom, but also claims and commissions them, to confess that they are hearers of His Word within the world and humanity which has not heard it but for which His work is dumb, and in this way to make the world and humanity hear.[7]

Patrick learned on Slemish mountain to trust in the ongoing salvific movement of the Triune God in the world, a lesson that we most certainly need to learn in Cascadia again today. What if we learned to measure the faithfulness of our activity not in the usual Christendom checklist of "noses and nickels" but rather in the effectiveness of our equipping the saints for their witness in the world?

Through my work directing the Centre of Missional Leadership at St. Andrew's Hall, Vancouver, I am always keen to connect with those who are discovering signs of the Holy Spirit's movement in our region. One of those connections put me in touch with Brandon Bailey, who pastors Tidelands Church in Stanwood, Washington. Visiting Brandon is a real treat as you hear the story of support from the Presbyterian Church down the road in Marysville who helped plant this new community of faith. Tidelands was designed as a missional community with the vision of gathering disciples and welcoming pre-Christian friends around a meal every Sunday night for the sake of equipping their witness in the world. Instead of consuming members' time, talent, and treasure to prop up the church institution,

5. Rogers, *St. Patrick*, 28.

6. Barth, *Church Dogmatics*, IV, III, 2 paragraph 71.

7. Barth, *Church Dogmatics* IV, 576. Barth also cautioned elsewhere that "It is not Jesus Christ who needs our ministries; it is our ministries that need Jesus Christ."

however, the model of ministry ensures that disciples are constantly turned out to the world—encouraged and equipped to live out their devotion to Christ in their workplace and neighborhoods.

For those who join the community as school teachers, the first thought is not, "Oh good, now we have a Sunday school teacher," but rather how can we help equip you to be a "faithful Christian witness within the pressure and limitations of the public school system?" Another member of their Christian fellowship has been commissioned to lead a Bible study in their government workplace over the lunch hour once a week rather than in a church building on a weekday night. Over time, as the community has multiplied, they've added a Sunday morning gathering in addition to their Sunday night meals, for the sake of equipping their people for witness. As they searched for space to gather for worship in Stanwood, Brandon heard of a place up for sale that had been several different things in recent years, from a mechanic's garage to a yoga studio. When he called the real estate agent to check it out the realtor replied casually, "Oh, so you want to have a look at the old Presbyterian Church?" Brandon was surprised. "The old Presbyterian Church?" he said. "Yes," the realtor replied, "that building was the Presbyterian Church in town until it dwindled and closed in the 1920s." Brandon had never heard of the former Presbyterian Church in this small town before. When he went to tour the property it felt like the perfect place for a new church plant. The missional community loved the old architecture and set about fixing it up for their ministry needs. When I visited the community, I thought about those faithful Christians in the 1920s, turning the lights out for the last time and likely feeling deflated and defeated with great sadness in their hearts. If someone told them back in the 1920s that a hundred years later a group of young Presbyterians—looking, worshipping and organizing themselves in a different way—would be filling the space day after day in praise of the Triune God they surely would not have believed it. Perhaps they would have thought it like an idle tale from women returning from an empty tomb.

God's "continuing conversion of the church" (to borrow Darrell Guder's language) should both unsettle us in our desire for measuring success by the world's standards, as well as give us hope for whatever seeds our witness may have—whether they bear fruit in our lifetime or not. In my pastoral care course at Regent College, I assign Andrew Purves's work *The Crucifixion of Ministry* for its refreshingly clear reminder of the source of power in ministry. Purves checks our need for approval by the current culture's standards of success when he argues, "Ministry kills us with regard to our ego needs, desire for power and success and the persistent wish to feel competent and in control."[8] To further drive home his point, Purves illustrates human limitations in ministry that instead forces us to rely on the Holy Spirit's power:

> It does not take us long to discover that we cannot heal the sick, raise the dead, calm the demonized, guide the morally afflicted, sober up the alcoholic, make the wife beater loving, calm the anxious, pacify the conflicted, control the intemperate, have answers to all the "Why?" questions, give the teenagers a moral compass and preach magnificent sermons every week, all the while growing the congregation and keeping the members happy.[9]

Purves reminds us that as Christian leaders we must fully rely on the presence and power of the Triune God at work in the world in order to be fruitful and faithful in ministry. This is especially difficult for churches emerging out of a Christendom legacy, where it was easy to point to programs and buildings, "noses and nickels," as a way of verifying that *their ministry* was successful. We middle or upper-class mainline Christians in the West, have become trapped in what I have referred to elsewhere as "the Laodicean captivity of the church," whereby too often we have domesticated the cutting edge of the gospel for the sake of our comfort and affluence and "encouraged and enabled an entitlement mentality regarding membership in the church."[10] A few years ago Michael Frost warned of how a post-Christendom church would live within a different paradigm of faithfulness.

> When we have no impressive buildings and no swollen budgets to sustain our work, often only then do we realize that the best we have to offer this post-Christendom world is the quality of our relationships, the power of our trustworthiness, and the wonder of our generosity. . . . Is it too simplistic to say that we earn that right [to be heard] through our authentic lifestyles? In a culture yearning for authenticity—the real—the pressure is on us in the Christian community now more than ever to put our time and money where our mouth is and live what we preach.[11]

8. Purves, *Crucifixion of Ministry*, xxi.

9. Purves, *Crucifixion of Ministry*, xxi.

10. Lockhart, *Lessons from Laodicea*, 36.

11. Frost, *Exiles*, 99. While I appreciate Frost's intention to have Christian witness connected to authentic lifestyle, I am cautious (as any good Calvinist might be) about our ability for self-deception due to sin. Authenticity is a double-edged sword.

Reaching back into the last century, Karl Barth could detect the warning signs of the end of Christendom and encouraged Christian witness that was bold and free from the metrics of Western culture. Barth wrote that a Christian would not, "allow himself to be disturbed by questions of minorities or majorities, of success or failure, of the probable or more likely improbable progress of Christianity in the world."[12] Instead, Barth says a witness of Jesus Christ will simply do and no more is required, "though, this is indeed required—that which he can do to proclaim the Gospel in his own age and place and circle, doing it with humility and good temper, but also with the resoluteness which corresponds to the great certainty of his hope in Jesus Christ."[13] Once again, we see how a missionary like St. Patrick to a pre-Christian society can be a source of encouragement and inspiration as we unlearn the ways of Christendom and attempt to offer a faithful witness to Jesus in this new context. Perhaps we need our own mountaintop moment with God, our sanctified Slemish encounter with the Triune God.

Several years ago while on pulpit exchange with a Presbyterian Church in Ireland congregation, I took my two older children Emily and Jack for a hike up Slemish mountain. We parked the car and started up the trail. Coming from the North Shore of Vancouver with its soaring snow capped mountains, my kids were less than impressed with this "little hill," as they called it. I had a healthy stash of Marks and Spencer's treats to bribe the children if need be, but they quickly zoomed ahead of me. After a half an hour of climbing, we stood at the top of Slemish mountain and took in the breathtaking view all around us. Marveling at the green fields stretching out as far as the eye could see, we sat down on the mountaintop and began eating our M & S Percy Pig gummies. With a deep sense of being on holy ground, I told my children the story of the young sixteen-year-old boy who once kept sheep beneath our feet and how God spoke to him in a way that changed his life, and changed the world.

Returning home months later to the North Shore of Vancouver, I laced up my hikers and travelled the short distance to the base of Grouse Mountain, home to the legendary Grouse Grind—known affectionately as "Mother Nature's Treadmill." The Grind is a rugged two-mile practically vertical climb on a trail of rocks and mud surrounded by soaring Douglas fir and cedar trees. The first few steps of Vancouver's Grouse Grind are deceptively easy. Within minutes, however, the mountainside pilgrimage steepens considerably. With

12. Barth, *Church Dogmatics*, IV.3.2, 919.
13. Barth, *Church Dogmatics*, IV.3.2, 919.

sweat trickling down my brow, I reflected on our latest trip to Ireland and my curiosity about the Island's most famous saint.

Perhaps like St. Patrick tending sheep on Slemish Mountain, I expected a moment of sudden revelation. Yes, that was it. Revelation. After all, God clearly has a desire to know and be known by God's creatures. "I will walk among you and be your God and you shall be my people," declares the Lord.[14] And yet, in Cascadia, it is common for people to admire nature without a Creator. *Vancouver Sun* religion and ethics reporter Douglas Todd suggests in *Cascadia: The Elusive Utopia* that a West Coast phenomenon has people putting nature before God. Todd argues that the intense individualism of those who live in Oregon, Washington State, and British Columbia, coupled with distrust of institutions generally, causes them to shun formal religion. Instead, there's nature, and environmental activism.

"It's a West Coast cliché, but when many residents of Cascadia want to find God, peace of mind, or just release from stress, they go for a walk in the forest or on the beach," Todd writes.[15] He notes that religious trends on the West Coast can often predict general trends across the continent. "However loosely, spirituality and nature are inextricably linked in the public's mind. . . . Call it a civil religion."[16]

So there I was, grinding my way up Grouse Mountain, soaking in the beauty of creation and longing to hear the voice of Patrick declare, "I arise today in power's strength, invoking the Trinity . . . in Sun's brightness, in Moon's radiance, in Fire's glory, in Wind's swiftness, in Sea's depth, in Rock's fixity." As my hiking boot kicked up some loose stones, I reflected on the Celtic church's ability to fuse a respect for creation with an abiding love of the Trinity. As a recovering sinner and someone always in the process of becoming Christian, this has served me as both faithful guide and companion.

Passing a makeshift memorial for a hiker who suffered a fatal heart attack on the Grind, I reflected on how God also provides such meaning for life, death and life beyond death. This Trinity—revealer, revealed and revealing—transforms us in community and mends this broken world. James B. Torrance argues that the Christian doctrine of the Trinity is the grammar of our participatory understanding of worship and prayer:

---

14. Lev 26: 12, *NRSV*.

15. Todd, *Cascadia*, 19.

16. Ibid.

Christ is presented to us as the Son living a life of union and communion with the Father in the Spirit, presenting himself in our humanity through the eternal Spirit to the Father on behalf of humankind. By his Spirit he draws men and women to participate both in his life of worship and communion with the Father and in his mission from the Father to the world.[17]

Our participation in the Trinity's union and communion shapes us for our participation in God's ongoing mission in the world of redemption and the reconciliation of the nations. Our joyful response to God's revelation in Jesus involves something more than belief, it moves us to something deeper: trust. Trust in the Triune God is what Patrick's story evokes. Trust from the time of Patrick's call on Slemish mountain as a slave through the rest of his life as he returned to Ireland with freedom in Christ to share. Patrick's trust in God also influenced others who would become, in time, fellow Hibernian saints. St. Columbanus once preached, "A road is to be walked upon and not lived in, so that they who walk upon it may dwell finally in the land that is their home." St. Brigit walked that road by feeding the poor at personal risk. St. Brendan and friends set out on a voyage seeking the will of God "as wandering pilgrims all the days of our lives." Trust and risk. At times, our contemporary expression of Christianity in North America lacks both.

Reaching the apex of the Grouse Grind, I soaked in the distant view of soaring skyscrapers, graceful bridges, and ocean grandeur. I thought of Patrick on that windswept mountain praying a hundred prayers by day and a hundred prayers by night. All our prayers are a fumbling response to God's grace-filled invitation to a relationship of mutual, self-giving love as revealed in Father, Son and Holy Spirit. I gave God thanks for life-transforming revelation at Slemish long ago and, by grace, God's ongoing revelation right here and right now in Cascadia. With a forest-covered mountain all around me, I remembered the shepherd turned saint and offered my own whispered prayers, joining with the Celtic Christians of old who declared:

Let us adore the Lord,

Maker of marvellous works,

Bright heaven with its angels,

And on earth the white-waved sea.[18]

---

17. Torrance, *Worship, Community and the Triune God of Grace*, 30–31.

18. A ninth-century Irish prayer quoted in Miller, *Celtic Devotions*, 48.

CHAPTER THREE

Uillula

Homesick at Home

To be elect in Christ Jesus, and there is no other election, means to be incorporated into his mission to the world, to be the bearer of God's saving purpose for his whole world, to be the sign and the agent and the first fruit of his blessed kingdom which is for all.

—LESSLIE NEWBIGIN, *THE GOSPEL IN A PLURALIST SOCIETY*

KIDNAPPED AT SIXTEEN YEARS old, Patrick spent six long, lonely years tending sheep on Slemish Mountain. Away from family and friends, with little hope of rescue or restoration to a normal life, Patrick shed his childhood "cultural Christianity" and began to pray to the living God revealed in Jesus Christ. Philip Freeman imagines a young Patrick once laughing at priests in Britain behind their backs and rolling his eyes with friends during church services he was forced to attend, "but now, with the cold wind biting his face and the never-ending rain soaking his skin, the idea of a God who loved and cared for his own took on a new appeal."[1] Alone and afraid, Patrick's dormant spirituality came alive through the Holy Spirit and the shepherd slave recalled vividly the biblical stories and prayers of his childhood. Patrick wrote in his *Confession* that while at Slemish he prayed a hundred prayers in the morning and another hundred prayers at night. How odd this newly devout teenager must have appeared to those around him. And what a powerful witness to the comforting and converting power

1. Freeman, *St. Patrick of Ireland*, 29.

17

of the Triune God Patrick must have been in that harsh and foreign land. As Freeman argues, "Since prayer in the ancient world was usually said out loud, the other members of the household, free and slave, must have noticed this change in behavior."[2]

Later in life, Patrick sat down to write his *Confession* and in it recalls this time of slavery in terms of God's first calling on his life. He wrote, "But it was here in Ireland that God first opened my heart, so that—even though it was a late start—I became aware of my failings and began to turn with my whole heart to the Lord my God."[3] Over six years, the Triune God drew Patrick into a loving relationship amidst the suffering and humiliation of this privileged Briton turned Irish slave. Then suddenly, God's call in Patrick's life would take a dramatic shift. Patrick remembered it this way: "One night while I was sleeping, I heard a voice saying to me: 'You have fasted well—soon you will be going home.' A short time after that I heard the voice again: 'Behold, your ship is ready.'"[4] Patrick risked his life by responding to God's call and left his master's farm, travelling 200 miles to a port where he was first denied boarding and then suddenly offered a crew position on a departing ship. What follows is a colorful tale of sailors in peril that seems to echo Paul's witness in Acts 27, a script that reads something like this: a faithful Christian, without power in the presence of pagans, places his trust in the Triune God that results in God's providential care for all. For Patrick, the providential care came in the form of a curious herd of wild boars provided for the ship's crew to eat just when all hope seemed to be exhausted. The provision (like manna in the wilderness) demonstrated to the pagan crew the reality and power of the God that Patrick worshipped while wandering through a desolate place somewhere in Britain. Most importantly, God led Patrick eventually home to Bannaventa Berniae. The Latin term that Patrick used in his later writing for the family home, Uillula, suggested that he was returning to a place of reasonable economic means and his family were of a relatively well to do social class.[5]

Imagine the scene. It would be like those milk cartons in the 1980s featuring a missing child juxtaposed with a computer-generated sketch of

2. Freeman, *St. Patrick of Ireland*, 29.

3. Patrick, *Confession*, Section 2.

4. Patrick, *Confession*, Section 17.

5. K. R. Dark, "St. Patrick's Uillula and the Fifth-Century Occupation of Romano-British Villas," in Dumville, *St. Patrick*, 19. While Uillula could refer to everything from farm to estate to hill fort, given Patrick's socio-economic background and family's standing in the community, this Uillula was more likely a formal, enclosed site.

what the lost boy might look like now. Six years after captivity, the lost boy is gone, replaced by this lean, strong young man who walks confidently into Bannaventa Berniae—the prodigal son returns home. What a party. What a celebration. What tears of joy and thanksgiving shed by Patricius's parents and the whole community. Questions abound. Where were you held in captivity? What did you do while six years a slave? How did you escape and make it back home? Servants approach respectfully, "Sir, did you see my sister taken on that same night?" Joy and sorrow mingle in the community. Slowly, Patricius returns to life as normal in Britain. And yet . . . Patrick is a changed man. No longer the young, rebellious cultural Christian in Roman Britain, he is now a young adult with a passionate faith in the risen Christ and practitioner of deep prayer. In a sense, he's home in Britain but no longer at home. Manitoba author Miriam Toews captures this teenage restlessness brilliantly in her book *A Complicated Kindness*. Toews places upon the lips of her teenage character, Nomi, stuck in a small town with her doleful father Ray, "Being seasick at sea is not the same as being homesick at home." *Homesick at home.* That's Patrick. And it's something his parents or old friends could never understand. And then God shows up again.

Not on the windswept mountains of Slemish, but this time a messenger of the Triune God shows up while Patrick is comfortably tucked into bed at night in Britain. Patrick later records the moment in this way:

> One night I was at home I saw a vision while sleeping—it was a man named Victoricus, coming to me as if he were arriving from Ireland. With him he brought a huge number of letters. He gave me one of them, and I saw that the first words were, "The Voice of the Irish." When I began to read this letter, all of a sudden I heard the voices of those Irish who lives near the woods of Foclut near the Western Sea. They called out to me with a single voice: "We beg you, holy boy, come here and walk among us!" I felt my heart breaking and was not able to read any more—and so I woke up. But thanks be to God, because after many years the Lord made their prayer come true.[6]

Vox Hibernia—the voice or call of the Irish. Later tradition has presented Victoricus as an angel, but it is more likely that Victoricus was simply another Roman slave that Patrick knew in captivity. Hibernia—the Roman name for Ireland—literally meaning the ends of the earth. A part of the earth that the Romans had never been able to conquer with military

---

6. Patrick, *Confession*, Section 23.

might. Now, from the ends of the earth comes a call for Patrick to return and minister amongst his former oppressors. Even the title of "holy boy" reeks of derision, a mocking title given by other slaves to this young shepherd soaked with the Holy Spirit on Slemish mountain. Yet, like John Wesley, the great revivalist who was first given the unkind nickname "Methodist" by his detractors, this "holy boy" of Britain would prove to be just that as he was soon to become the apostle to the Irish. The twelfth-century Cistercian monk Jocelin enthusiastically describes Patrick's response to *Vox Hibernia* in this way

> And Patrick, being pierced therewith in his heart, could not finish the letter, but awaking gave infinite thanks to God; for he was assured by the vision, that the Lord had set him apart from his Mother's womb, had by his grace called him to convert and save the Irish nation, which seemed to desire his presence among them.[7]

God's call, and recall, returns again and again in other visions that Patrick records, such as "I heard the most beautiful words, a prayer—but I couldn't understand what was being said. Only God knows if the words were coming from inside me or were somewhere beyond me." Patrick continues by describing the prayer as follows: "The one who gave his life for you, it is he who speaks in you," giving him the assurance of the next faithful step, "and I awoke full of joy."[8]

Patrick's "Vox Hibernia" leads him away from the comforts of home to theological education and missional leadership in Ireland for the rest of his life. Hearing Patrick's call to minister amongst a hostile pre-Christian people leads us to wonder what a "*Vox Cascadia*" might look like—a call to minister amongst an apathetic post-Christian people.

Reflection on God's call in our lives and the electrifying reality of God's election is a necessary step towards missional leadership in a post-Christian society, where messaging about Christian leadership has often turned negative, both inside and outside the church.[9] My friend and colleague Richard Topping explored this theme in the 2015 Niblett Lecture at Sarum College, building on an earlier argument from Will Willimon, when he argued

7. Swift, *The Life and Acts of Saint Patrick*, 29.

8. Patrick, *Confession*, Section 24.

9. I recall being interviewed for ministry many years ago by a Presbytery student committee and being told, "You seem like a smart young man, are you sure you want to enter ministry, perhaps medicine or law would be a better fit?" Lord, have mercy.

What happens when a young person comes to a priest or minister with a sense that God may be "speaking to me." In Canada, the clergy might ask, "Did you have a fight with your parents? What did you have for dinner last night?" or "Is everything ok with your partner?" God becomes a last resort if education and formation are too accommodationist to the immanent frame. Followed to its logical conclusion pastoral theology becomes techniques for success, managerial tips, and tricks for effective ministry; a kind of atheism that ministers as though God doesn't matter and imaginative formation in the gospel to attend to the works and ways of God among us recedes. Secularity has also reduced the cultural prestige associated with ministerial or priestly office in Canada. This break with power is a liberty since with the sociological props kicked out, ministry can actually be theologically guided for prophetic critique—if it resists the methadone of other sociological and cultural prescriptions. However, awareness of ministry as a calling has fallen off the radar screen and the impression of ministers as "quivering masses of availability" who want to help people (Hauerwas) or "patient guardians of the status quo" (Willimon), rather than impatient instigators, does not get us the right people. Recruitment of suitably gifted candidates is a crisis.[10]

Listening for God's call in our lives and trusting in God's election for the sake of the world often gets bogged down in a misunderstanding of the doctrine of election known often as "predestination." I recall several years ago sitting at the Europa hotel in downtown Belfast with colleagues from Newry Presbytery on a lunch break from the General Assembly. We were all telling our favorite Presbyterian jokes and it was only a matter of time until predestination came up. One preacher told the story of a Presbyterian who died and went to heaven. He was a little surprised that instead of waking to see the pearly gates he saw instead a fork in the road. On one sign it read, "Predestination." On the other, "Free Will." Naturally, the Presbyterian selected the path labeled predestination. Eventually he found himself before a huge, wooden door. He reached up for the giant brass knocker and gave it a good bang. The door opened a crack and an angel stood before him. "Mortal, how did you end up at this door?" Without thinking the man said, "I chose this path." "*You* chose it?" said the angel with obvious disgust and promptly slammed the door in the Presbyterian's face. The man was so discouraged so he wandered back to

10. Topping, "Troubling Context," 49. In this section of the article, Topping draws on Willimon, "The Goal of Seminary," 12.

the fork in the road, shrugged his shoulders and walked down the path of "Free will." In short course he came to another large, wooden door and knocking it, the door opened a crack and another angel stood before him. "Mortal, how did you end up at this door of free will?" The man looked sadly at the angel and said, "I had no choice."

Recovering a healthy understanding of God's call and election for the mission of the church in post-Christendom is essential. The Triune God, acting out of complete sovereignty, makes the choice to welcome us with covenant love expressed through perichoretic participation in the communion of Father, Son, and Holy Spirit. Election reminds us that God is on a mission in this world to create, redeem, and sustain creation and all created things for his own good purposes. Ironically, predestination in this context is not set against free will, like the joke with the fork in the road. Instead, it is quite the opposite. Because God freely chooses humankind, adopts us as children of light and faith, we are truly free to live as God's people in the world. God's free choice enables our free will. As Will Willimon says, "God's Word to us is God's will for us."[11] Election reminds us of the gracious, saving presence of God in the world. Sadly, too many of our Christian communities lack evidence of this radical, life-changing action of the Triune God, as Willimon cautions:

> Perhaps election receives little attention in mainline Protestantism because our churches have limited ourselves to second hand believers, cradle Christians and those who cannot remember when they were not culturally Christian. By so limiting the scope of salvation to the heirs of the previously committed, we have confused people into thinking that they are in church on the basis of their astute choices or as the beneficiaries of skilled parenting. Is much of mainline church life boring, are many of my sermons flat because we lack invigorating, empty-handed, grateful, recent converts whose presence among us is testimony to the reality of election?[12]

Patrick's movement from cultural Christianity through conversion to call as a minister of the gospel is an example of Christ's calling for apostolic witness in the world that continues today. Early in Mark's Gospel we read, "Jesus went up on a mountainside and called to him those he wanted, and they came to him. He appointed twelve designating them apostles—that they

11. Willimon, *How Odd of God,* 38.
12. Ibid., 35.

might be with him and that he might send them out to preach and to have authority to drive out demons."[13] What good news that Jesus calls *us* to be equipped to be sent out as apostles. We are invited into the school of Jesus that we might graduate from disciple to apostle for the sake of joining God in the healing of the nations. Election is not about hoarding our soteriological treasure for our own sake but a celebration of God's call upon our lives for the sake of the world. Perhaps that's why Karl Barth opens *Church Dogmatics* II/2 with such a bold statement that the election of grace (his preferred language for predestination) is the whole summary of the gospel.

Of course, when we hear the story of Patrick's call in *Vox Hibernia* it is a curious echo of another Apostle's call to minister in a foreign land. The book of Acts records it this way

> Paul and his companions traveled throughout the region of Phrygia and Galatia, having been kept by the Holy Spirit from preaching the word in the province of Asia. When they came to the border of Mysia, they tried to enter Bithynia, but the Spirit of Jesus would not allow them to. So they passed by Mysia and went down to Troas. During the night Paul had a vision of a man of Macedonia standing and begging him, "Come over to Macedonia and help us." After Paul had seen the vision, we got ready at once to leave for Macedonia, concluding that God had called us to preach the gospel to them.[14]

God as an active agent of salvation is common in both of these call stories of Paul and Patrick. God breaks into their lives for his own good purposes. For Paul, the Council in Jerusalem is over and he is ready to get out on the missionary trail. Paul has a wee falling out with Barnabas over John Mark and ends up adding Timothy as a missionary partner. The plan is to revisit places where Paul has already preached but the strangest thing happens. Paul has a plan and God's plan is different, imagine that. Has that ever happened in your life? Where might there be faithful Christians in Cascadia or beyond whose plans have not worked out and who need encouragement for their witness? How might God be communicating with them in our time and place? How might we, like St. Patrick, tell our life story in a way that re-presents the biblical witness and stories in new ways in our lives?

Paul intends to go deep into the Roman province of Asia. That language confuses us today for when we hear Asia we think of jumping on a

13. Mark 3:13, *NIV*.

14. Acts 16: 6–10, *NIV*.

Cathay Pacific flight. Instead, Asia was the name of the Roman province for what we call Turkey today. So, Paul plans to go to Turkey but he gets as far as Mysia and wants to turn north to Bithynia (that's roughly where Istanbul is today). *But the spirit of Jesus prevents him from going any farther.* What? Here is someone out on the missionary trail, wanting to proclaim the gospel and God is stopping him? What is that about? Calvin suggests evidence of election when he writes:

> Why did the Lord forbid Paul to speak in Asia, and did not allow him to come into Bithynia? . . . There is nothing better than to leave God the freedom and power to deem those, whom He pleases, worthy of His grace, or deprive them of it. And certainly since His eternal election is of grace, so must the calling, which flows from it, be considered of grace, and it is not founded on men, since it owes nothing to anyone. Accordingly, let us realize that the Gospel comes forth to us from the one foundation of pure grace.[15]

God had a different plan. God had a better plan. God inconvenienced Paul for a purpose. Instead, Paul goes farther west to Troas, roughly where the ancient city of Troy was located. Paul goes to sleep discouraged. Have you felt discouragement like that in your ministry? Things have not turned out in your life as you planned? You may have even felt that you were doing God's work and yet nothing seemed to work as you imagined? Well, then you know how Paul felt. What good news to realize that God doesn't just call once. God calls us again and again and again. Paul in this story from the book of Acts is being re-called. He goes to sleep and has a dream . . . a vision . . . as the Bible calls it. A man stands there and says, "Come over to Macedonia and help us." Without hesitation Paul gets up and heads to Macedonia. Why is this important? This is the first time Paul preaches the gospel in Europe; just imagine the impact of that ministry over the last 2,000 years. When you visit the region of ancient Neopolis in Greece today there is the beautiful church of St. Nicholas with mosaic tiles on the outside that depict the Macedonian call and Paul's first visit to Europe. On the left-hand side of the mural you see Paul curled up in Troas hearing the call, in the middle a soldier-like gentleman in the middle issuing the call, and on the right, Paul points a toe out of a boat reaching for the shore and marking the moment the gospel arrives in Europe. This "re-call" from God changed the world. So too, God's recall of Patrick to Ireland in the Vox Hibernia moment changed the future of an island and a people. Lesslie Newbigin

15. Torrance, eds., *Calvin's Commentaries*, 68–69.

reminds us that this call, this election, is for the sake of the whole world by drawing us into God's missional dream of redemption:

> The mission of the Church to all the nations, to all human communities in all their diversity and in all their particularity, is itself the might work of God, the sign of the inbreaking of the kingdom. The Church is not so much the agent of the mission as the locus of the mission. It is God who acts in the power of the Spirit, doing mighty works, creating sings of a new age, working secretly in the hearts of men and women to draw them to Christ. When they are so drawn, they become part of a community which claims no masterful control of history, but continues to bear witness to the real meaning and goal of history by a life which—in Paul's words—by always bearing about in the body the dying of Jesus becomes the place where the risen life of Jesus is made available for others.[16]

God's call sets us free from our past and points us towards a future shaped by the gospel. The apostle Paul understood that. Patrick, a slaved turned missionary understood that. Karl Barth once remarked, preaching to prisoners in Basel, that his sin, captivity and suffering were yesterday's realities and not in the present moment. Barth continued that his sins are, "of my past, not of the present nor of the future. I have been saved! Look once again to Jesus Christ in his death upon the cross. Look and try to understand that what he did and suffered he did for you, for me, for all of us. He carried our sin . . . we are saved by no other than Jesus Christ, we are saved by grace."[17] God's election is not to "puff Christians up" but rather we are elect to be equippers, saved to be sent, called to be commissioned as Christ's witnesses to the ends of the earth. While God's covenant and election is focused on a few, it is always for the sake of the world.[18] How might we understand our role in a post-Christendom context as the sent people of God in the world Christ died to save?

16. Newbigin, *The Gospel in a Pluralist Society*, 118–19.

17. Barth, *Deliverance to the Captives*, 39.

18. Goheen, ed., *Reading the Bible Missionally*, 27.

CHAPTER FOUR

Auxerre

Theological Education

*"More important than our experience of Christ
is the Christ of our experience."*

—JAMES B. TORRANCE, *WORSHIP, COMMUNITY
AND THE TRIUNE GOD OF GRACE*

FOLLOWING PATRICK'S VOX HIBERNIA experience, details are a little vague
on his next most faithful step towards becoming a missionary Bishop for
Ireland. While opinion varies, it is generally thought that Patrick left Britain
to be trained for more formal Christian leadership in the Roman province
of Gaul. Some believe he went first to study at the monastery of Lerins, on
an island off the southeast coast of France. Patrick would have studied for
a time there with Honoratus, where it is said the future Irish saint developed his character of charity and humility and "learnt to appreciate their
beauty in the character of Honoratus and in his divinity school at Lerins."[1]
At some point it is most likely that he was sent to Auxerre, France where
he studied under Saint Germanus. Consecrated bishop on July 7, 418,
Germanus took up his episcopal duties from his predecessor St. Amator,
who departed this world with a series of notable, miraculous events that
included the presence of an angel choir and a paralytic healed by the
command of Germanus. It is believed that during that same year, Patrick
came to place himself under Bishop Germanus's guidance. Germanus
and Patrick appeared to have much in common: "there was one devotion

1. Hitchcock, *St. Patrick and His Gallic Friends*, 125.

practiced by St. Germanus with which St. Patrick had long been familiar. It is recorded of the Bishop of Auxerre that he, like our saint, was frequently accustomed to spend the entire night in prayer."[2] In the fifth century there were no formal seminaries as we might know them today associated with, or on, the campuses of major secular universities. Patrick's path towards ministry would have been a long and arduous journey of study, mentoring, service, and personal reflection. The method of his training, that continued well into the Middle Ages, meant that preparation for ordained ministry consisted in being mentored by other clergy as to how the liturgy was to be celebrated and the duties that were expected of a cleric at the time.[3] But what was Patrick taught theologically speaking?

In his *Confession*, Patrick describes the Creed that he was taught and shared with the Irish in the course of his ministry. Irish priest Jim Mc-Cormack has updated Patrick's words in a Eugene Peterson-like *Message* style to convey to contemporary listeners the basic creedal teaching during Patrick's study for the priesthood

> This is what we were taught: There is no other God, past, present or to come, than the Father who has always been, without beginning; from whom is all beginning; holding all things together. And we profess that his Son Jesus Christ along with the Father has most certainly always existed before the world began; and to have been generated in the Father's Being, before all beginnings, in a way that is beyond our understanding; and through the Son all things came to be; both what we see, as well as things too deep for our gaze. He became a human being. And when death had been overthrown, was taken up to the heavens to be with the Father, who gave him all power over everything that can be named on the earth, in the heavens, and in the underworld. So let every voice confess to the Father that Jesus Christ is Lord and God. We believe in him and look forward to his return in the near future, as judge of the living and the dead, to deal with everyone as their deeds deserve. And God lavished the gift of the Spirit on us as the guarantee that we would inherit with Christ, and live forever. For it is the Spirit who forms those who believe and are obedient to God, into his children. We profess our faith in this One God, of three-fold sacred name. And we worship him.[4]

2. Cusack, *The Life of St. Patrick*, 166.

3. Swan, *The Experience of God in the Writings of Saint Patrick*, 25.

4. McCormack, *St. Patrick*, 11–12.

This chapter of Patrick's *Confession* is known as the "Rule of Faith" of the British Church by some scholars who note that the churches in Gaul and Britain "borrowed its Rule of Faith from bishop Victorinus early in the forth century but . . . enlarged this summary during the forth century to admit clauses designed to exclude Arianism," a form of unitarian heresy denying the Trinity in favor of God the Father's supremacy over Christ and the Spirit.[5] As a result, this part of the *Confession* is written in Latin far more polished than Patrick's own work and clearly expresses an orthodox view of "God's three acts of love: first in creation, the second in sending Jesus Christ to redeem the world, the third in giving us the Holy Spirit as the giver of light and life."[6]

Patrick would also have engaged in systematic and sustained study of Scripture. While having missed significant education in Latin between the critical ages of sixteen and twenty-two years due to captivity in Ireland, he would have been expected to keep up with the other theological students as they worked with the Latin Bible in their studies. From the *Confession*, it is clear that he had a firm grasp of the Holy Scriptures, leading D. R. Howlett to conclude, "Patrick was a *homo unius libria* 'a man of one book,' he had read, marked, learned and inwardly digested that book. He appropriated not only the words, but the inner meanings and habits of thought he had found in the Latin Bible and internalized them to a remarkable degree."[7]

Patrick's creedal, biblical theological education equipped him for an orthodox evangelistic ministry to Ireland. The catechism by which he was formed would help him to translate the gospel into a new culture as he crossed from the Roman world back into the context of Hibernia. Raymond Herbenick summarizes Patrick's theological approach in this way:

> St Patrick seems to have formulated a lyrical catechism as a legacy to the Irish peoples with affirming and hospitable instruction in the positive content of a Celtic Christian faith in Ireland rather than an inhospitable and demeaning apologetic. This legacy included warmth in the words of a welcoming Tongue that is free theologically from the Arian distortions of the Triune Godhead and free ethically from the Pelagian distortion of an omnipotent human agency without the need for God's grace.[8]

5. Hanson, *The Life and Writings of the Historical Saint Patrick*, 53.

6. Whiteside, *The Spirituality of St. Patrick*, 21.

7. Howlett, *The Book of Letters of Saint Patrick the Bishop*, 11.

8. Herbenick, *On the Erudition of the Historical St. Patrick*, 83. Two common heresies of the early church: Arianism that subordinated Christ to the Father making him a junior

Patrick would have been around thirty years old when he completed his initial training and was ordained a deacon. "Priested" a few years later, some believe he may have been nearly fifty years old by the time he was consecrated bishop. For many, the debate is whether he was sent to Ireland first as a missionary priest or a missionary bishop. Unfortunately, there really is no way to verify whether he was made a bishop before his mission to Ireland or during his mission to Hibernia.

During his years of study in Auxerre, however, Patrick presented himself as an unusual student. As a young adult convert to Christianity, Patrick missed critical years of formal education due to his captivity in Ireland. Patrick was keenly aware his whole life that his missing education set him at a disadvantage within the wider church and was a source of ridicule from others. As a result of these deficiencies, it is suspected that some of his religious superiors were reluctant to send him back to Ireland as a missionary.

Church officials were forced to change their mind, however, when word arrived that the King of Leinster banished Palladius, the first missionary bishop to Ireland, in 431 AD. Palladius went on to minister amongst the Scots in northern Britain and leadership for the fledgling mission to Hibernia was needed immediately. Opinion regarding what actually happened to Palladius varies, of course, with Muirchu's biography of Patrick contained in *The Book of Armagh* suggesting that Patrick, along with another priest Segitius, were on their way to Ireland when they received news of Palladius's death. The closest bishop to them was a man named Amatorex, who blessed their mission and consecrated Patrick to the office of bishop before he arrived in Ireland.[9] Defenders of Palladius claim that the power of Patrick's hagiography has exaggerated the failing of Palladius as the first missionary bishop to Hibernia in order to enhance Patrick's reputation. Whatever the timing of his ordination as Bishop, Patrick stood out as the one who the church needed as a witness to "the ends of the earth." Patrick knew both the language and culture in order to translate the gospel into the context of that strange and untamed land. It is believed, in fact, that Patrick spoke at least three languages. Patrick could communicate in Latin (despite being self-conscious regarding his limitations, due to missing his formal education while a slave in Ireland) as well as Q-Celtic (the modern languages of Irish, Manx, and Gallic) and P-Celtic (the modern languages of Welsh,

---

vice president in the Trinity, and Pelagianism that denied original sin.

9. Bieler, *The Patrician Texts in the Book of Armagh*, 5.

Cornish, and Breton).[10] The two branches of the Celtic language were quite different and unrecognizable to each other. Patrick would have learned P-Celtic growing up in Roman Britain and then acquired Q-Celtic while a slave in Ireland. As Thomas O'Loughlin remarks, "An Irish raider in Wales in the fifth century would not have understood the local inhabitants, nor vice versa, and would have had no fellow feeling on the basis of being 'fellow Celts.'"[11] Therefore, Patrick's presence at Auxerre was well timed with both a vacancy and a perceived sense of urgency to send a representative of the church who would be best equipped for witness in that most un-Roman culture of Hibernia. Prior to Patrick's sending to Ireland by Pope Celestine I, we are left to wonder about the details of how an established church within Christendom prepared a missionary for a world outside its experience, when even mission had begun to fall out of the Christian lexicon. As Stephan Paas reminds us, "Of course, there was a lot of work to be done in Christian countries, but to call this work 'mission' in the pure sense of the word was to deny the difference between pastoral work among baptized people on the one hand and missionary work among pagans on the other."[12] We know from Patrick's writings that this study for missionary work was a difficult and soul-searching time of preparation for ministry.[13] In many ways, that's the struggle that mainline churches in particular have when it comes to theological education in North America today.

There appears to be a looming crisis facing those attempting to equip the next generation of Christian leaders in the West. For many years now I have been involved with the Forum for Theological Education (FTE) as both a pastor and a professor. FTE, founded in 1954 by John D. Rockefeller, Jr. and others, was originally known as "The Fund for Theological Education." Their concern was the increasing awareness that young, bright Christians were pursing vocations outside of ministry, thus creating a talent

10. O'Loughlin, *Saint Patrick*, 28.

11. Ibid.

12. Paas, *Church Planting*, 82–83.

13. Prior to being ordained deacon, Patrick confessed a teenage sin to a friend also preparing for ministry. Patrick's contemporary, St. Augustine of Hippo, also confessed to childhood sins like stealing fruit, but it is believed that Patrick's sin was far more grievous. While never named by Patrick, it is believed that he murdered someone in his teen years, possibly even a slave on his family farm. The friend who heard Patrick's confession before ordination as deacon would later share that secret with church officials in an attempt to block his ordination as a missionary bishop. And yet, God used the brokenness of Patrick both in captivity and this colleague's betrayal to focus and sharpen his missional leadership gifts, as can still be read so clearly today in his *Confession*.

deficit in the church. Their response was to fund a "trial" year of theological education for the best and brightest of the next generation, in order to encourage some to consider the call to Christian leadership in the church for the sake of the world. Today, FTE is a theologically and ethnically diverse organization, funded generously by the Lilly Foundation, that seeks to actively identify and inspire passionate, diverse, talented young leaders to become pastoral leaders and theological educators. Now, as a member of the FTE board of trustees, I see the challenges and opportunities for noticing, naming, and nurturing the call to ministry for the future "Saint Patrick's or Patricia's" of the next generation. Just as St. Patrick entered a theological education system that was designed to equip leaders for a parish model system out of touch with the needs for missional leadership, so too today often our theological schools prepare future leaders for a church culture and context that no longer exists.

As director of the Centre for Missional Leadership at St. Andrew's Hall, our college is attempting to reshape the curriculum and method of theological education in order to produce missionaries for the post-Christian North American context. Our focus is on equipping inspired and inspiring missional leaders. One of the ways of achieving this goal is by reclaiming mission as a central theme of theological education.

For anyone who spends even a little time reflecting on theological education in the West, the name Fredrich Schleiermacher is sure to come up. Schleiermacher (1768–1834) was the son of a Prussian Army Chaplain who, like revivalist John Wesley, was deeply influenced by Moravian pietism. Schleiermacher wedded his "higher order Moravian pietism" with the Romanticism movement that pushed back against the rational theology of the Enlightenment. His famous *On Religion: Speeches to Its Cultured Despisers* critiques the Christian faith simply as knowing or doing and lands rather comfortably in the realm of feelings where, "religion is sense and taste for the Infinite."[14] As a Presbyterian, I feel twitchy whenever we lean too much on feelings, fearing that we are only moments away from someone calling for a "group hug." My students will tell you that, "Ross had an emotion twenty years ago—he didn't like it!" Despite this reservation, I believe Schleiermacher was responding faithfully to the tension between gospel and culture in his own context. His desire to make the Christian faith more accessible (or perhaps cynically one might say acceptable) to those around him is understandable. As a pastor in Cascadia, I cannot count the number

---

14. Schleiermacher, *On Religion*, 36.

of times I've been pressured to water down the gospel in order to make the strange claim that "a crucified Jew rules the cosmos" easier to accept at witty cocktail parties. But God's paradigm-shattering, world-shifting, life-changing event in the birth, life, ministry, passion, death, resurrection and ascension in Jesus Christ is not something that will ever be easy to explain away in order to curry favor with cultural elites.

My own sense of theological education's movement into the wilderness in the West has been shaped by scholars like Richard Osmer at Princeton Theological Seminary, who reminds us that Schleiermacher's response to the scientific emphasis in the nineteenth-century Western universities was to think of theology in similar logical patterns with three branches: philosophical theology, historical theology (where Schleiermacher placed dogmatics!), and practical theology. Flowing from this logic, theological education in the West increasingly subdivided its work into the now familiar silos of biblical, historical, theological, and practical studies. Osmer describes this move in theological education as having the following characteristics:

1. Theology is divided into specialized, relatively autonomous fields.

2. Each field pursues its distinctive tasks along the lines of a modern research discipline, with a specialized language, methods of inquiry, and subject matter.

3. The goal of theological scholarship is the production of knowledge.

4. The specific task of practical theology is to relate the scholarship of the other theological disciplines to the work of clergy and congregations.[15]

Kyle Small summarizes Protestant theological education as a modernity project (now held captive), suggesting it recognizes authority within the individual, not in external sources. Small argues, "Competition, linearity in curriculum, individualism, and political correctness locate authority in the autonomous individual, and all of them diminish any sense of moral authority in external or traditional sources."[16]

---

15. Osmer, *Practical Theology*, 234. Osmer argues that practical theology's four core tasks include the descriptive-empirical (what is going on?), the interpretive (why is this going on?), the normative (what ought to be going on?), and the pragmatic (how might we respond?).

16. Small, "Missional Theology for Schools of Theology," in Van Gelder, ed., *The Missional Church and Leadership Formation*, 63.

My colleague Richard Topping names the struggle for western theological education in an attempt to appear "relevant" to the secular university in Schleiermacher-like fashion. Topping states,

> Very often course descriptions from mainline theological institutions in Canada evidence a reserve with respect to God and divine agency in the world. God, when God appears in a course title, is often listed as a problem to be solved. Scripture interpretation becomes biblical studies through "synchronic historicism"; that is, by de-canonizing texts and placing them into a naturalized historical-cultural frame as their preponderant context. Postmodernism has made us quite aware of our perspectives on the world, one should be concerned that western or male or heterosexual lenses are not allowed to distort; but sometimes the adjunct disciplines which instruct such seeing so foreground a particular "perspective" that the subject matter of theology (God) is eclipsed. We end up studying lenses and not what is looked at. It makes me think of Karl Barth's comment—"theology is not anthropology [or sociology] in a really loud voice."[17]

In my teaching with Darrell Guder, I have heard him say many times that "missional" language is like scaffolding that (hopefully) one day can be removed. But, as long as theological education can speak about hermeneutics or soteriology or ecclesiology with no connection to the ongoing redemptive mission of the Triune God in the world, then we must always add the modifier "missional" in front of the theological area under discussion. Today, there appears to be a tug of war taking place between colleges and within faculties, as to whether one should lean more towards a so called "objective religious studies" approach to theological education in order to curry favor with the broader cultural establishment (perhaps a dying gasp and clutching after Christendom prestige) or tack instead in the direction of a closer commitment to the mission of the church in the proclamation of the gospel and formation of counter-cultural witnessing communities. While "either/or" statements invite gross over-generalizations, there does appear to be tension within theological education as the broader society secularizes and decisions have to be made with buildings, budgets, and endowments

---

17. Topping, "Troubling Context," 45. Later Topping notes that for too long theologians have bracketed out the faith in order to receive admission into the wider academy. He concludes, "The ticket price is too high, and this move is neither inevitable nor interesting since it mutes the particular contribution theologians and church leaders have to make to the life of the church, the university and . . . society."

regarding which direction to lean. Richard Osmer contends, "As Protestant-ism has become one religious community among many in a differentiated and pluralistic social context, it has been forced to rethink its relationship to public life generally."[18] This is especially hard with the former mainline denominational colleges that have relied on the cooperation and financial assistance of the broader culture—not just the hard working Marthas who send in the donations or the studious Marys who fill the classrooms, but the good will and support of the curious, onlooking crowd wondering from a distance what Rabbi Jesus might do next.[19]

In conversation on this tension, Darrell Guder has suggested that theological education faculties should be asking themselves questions like, "How has the context of their students changed since they became a profes-sor? How has the outward social context changed? How have these changes affected the teaching of your disciplines? How does every course at Semi-nary help equip the saints for their ministry?" Questions like these can help keep theological faculties in touch with the current realities and challenges of Christian witness and avoid what Lillian Daniel noted as seminary pro-fessors who wax eloquently about their vast pastoral experience of two years in a congregation, twenty years ago.[20] Instead, in the outcomes-driven model of North American theological education today, too many times a seminary education is deemed complete if the various competencies are checked off the list and outcomes achieved. Darrell Guder suggests instead that the best measure of a theological education is not assessed by outcomes at graduation, but rather by determining what quality and effectiveness of the community they are leading years later. Guder contends:

> The missional discussion may be properly understood as the con-tinuing theological investigation of the character and purposes of the missio Dei. Missional theology may be defined as Trinitar-ian missiocentricity. Parsing what that means is a task requiring rigorous work, embracing and affecting all of the theological disciplines.[21]

18. Osmer and Schweitzer, *Religious Education between Modernization and Global-ization,* 211.

19. John 11.

20. Daniel, "Spiritual Not Religious" lecture, Vancouver School of Theology convoca-tion 2016.

21. Guder, "Taking the Form of a Servant," Laidlaw Lectures, Knox College, March 11, 2015.

Where I am privileged to serve the church and prepare future leaders, the decision to stop chasing respectability from the broader university and focus instead on developing missional leaders for Christ's church has provided keen insights for theological education. St. Andrew's Hall exercises its charter through the Vancouver School of Theology, which recently sold it's iconic castle-like "Iona Building" to the University of British Columbia, constructing in its place a new, state-of-the-art, distance-learning building complete with a hipster coffee shop on the main floor. The change of location has also been accompanied by a renewed focus on preparing leaders for the church of post-Christendom rather than a maintenance-minded approach to institutional survival. St. Andrew's Hall contributes to teaching and resourcing this vision through the Centre for Missional Leadership. The decision to move away from the Christendom legacy that seeks cultural support and respectability for theological education frees one up to look again through a missional lens how best to teach the theological disciplines beyond Schleiermacher's nineteenth-century silos. While a deep dive into this conversation would require a monograph on its own, in order to spark imagination and discussion I will explore only three examples as a way to illustrate this shift towards preparing leaders for a post-Christendom context.

Missional Hermeneutics

The first area to explore is missional hermeneutics. Regarding the missional reform of theological education, Richard Topping argues, "This work . . . needs to extend across the whole of the theological curriculum and ought to center on attending to the Bible as Holy Scripture; that is, as testimony caught up in the divine economy of reconciliation."[22] Building on Richard Bauckham's work, Michael Goheen suggests that a missional hermeneutic has three key dimensions: reading the whole of Scripture with mission as its central theme, reading Scripture to understand what mission really means in the world today, and reading Scripture to equip the church for its missional task.[23] A missional curriculum both in the church and academy will take seriously that all the various subject areas are formed in both "content and purpose by this core which sees mission—defined as missionary encounter

22. Topping, "Troubling Context," 52.
23. Goheen, ed., *Reading the Bible Missionally*, 15.

between the gospel and the cultural story—as defining the church."[24] Darrell Guder contends that God enables apostolic missionaries to form witnessing communities from "generation to generation, from culture to culture, from language to language, and from polity to polity. Crucial to every generation and every cultural translation of the apostolic mandate is the biblical formation of the witnessing community."[25] For those of us in the formerly mainline church in particular, this focus on missional hermeneutics can expose how our shifting interpretation of Scripture presents particular hurdles to overcome in a post-Christendom context.

I first glimpsed the challenge of generations of mainline Christians raised on a steady diet of "higher criticism" of Scripture when I served as a youth pastor in Toronto. I can still picture the scene. The grease-stained pizza boxes were piled high in the corner of the room as youth group neared the halfway mark of the evening. A delightful assortment of teens chatted away, filling the tiny space with a cacophony of giggles, shouts, and cheers as an impromptu game of Nerf football broke out under a pencil sketch of "laughing Jesus." Aware of a looming deadline, I called the group to order. "Okay, it's time to plan the youth service that's coming up at the end of the month. Before we go any further tonight, we have to settle on a Bible story to focus our efforts. Any ideas?"

Silence. Then one brave hand went up. "Ross, why do we have to read from the Bible in church? Why can't we just read Dr. Seuss or a poem or something? What makes the Bible so special?" Many mainline churchgoers have voiced (or whispered) these honest questions over the years in our post-Enlightenment West. Why do we need to read the Bible in our public worship? Why the Bible and not some other spiritual resource? In many corners of the church, there has been a loss of confidence in the authority of the Bible.[26] Perhaps it has to do with a growing awareness of other sacred texts or the overall declining position of the church in society. I have a hunch, however, it is more than that. It may have something to do with what I call "TBS." Let me explain.

I love "Throwback Thursdays" on Facebook. The concept is simple: Post a "retro" photo of yourself or someone you know and delight in how

---

24. Goheen, ed., *Reading the Bible Missionally*, 314.

25. Guder, "The Implications of a Missional Hermeneutic for Theological Education," in Goheen, ed., *Reading the Bible Missionally*, 289.

26. One might argue that that we not only deny authority to the Bible but to any authority at all beyond ourselves!

much has changed. Be prepared, however, to take some good-natured rib-
bing about how you looked so long ago; anything from culture (huge cell
phones) to fashion (1980s zipper pants) to outrageous hairdos (um, can
you say rat tail or mullet?). Throwback Thursdays are a delightful way to
reflect on how much has changed over the years.

I've wondered lately, however, whether in our leadership preparation
for Christ's Church we are in danger of creating TBS, Throwback Sundays.
From coast to coast it is obvious that the 1950s are long gone—back when
the fumes of Christendom used the culture and social norms to encourage people's participation in local mainline churches. Today, when no one
is socially compelled to be involved in a worshipping community, we talk
about innovative, emerging, and missional leadership in the church, but
I worry sometimes that we are still too often preparing people for TBS,
Throwback Sundays.

For example, I have heard it said that the way we teach the Bible, whether in seminary on a Tuesday morning or a church lounge on a Wednesday
night, is primarily an attempt to break down a pre-critical understanding
of Scripture. In other words, to borrow from the teaching of hermeneutical
theorist Paul Ricoeur, what we need to do is to take people from their "first
naiveté" through "critical reflection" to a "second naiveté." Now, to be honest,
I love this language. As someone who strives to help form "scholarly evangelists" for Christ's church, I've been using Ricoeur's three steps for years in
teaching and preaching. The challenge is the assumption some people make
regarding the first naiveté that is found today in post-Christendom Canada.
For a long time now in seminary, the assumption has been that leaders
should assume that the first naiveté is a dogged, uncritical biblical literalism.
The educator's role, therefore, was to break that "naive" viewpoint in order
to lead people (and their worshipping communities) to a more nuanced and
historical-critical understanding of the Bible. I get that.

The "hermeneutics of suspicion" have brought us a long way from the
naiveté of the old days. But after pastoring congregations across a post-
Christendom country, I've found that the first naiveté is no longer biblical literalism. Most pre-Christian people I interact with at the coffee shop,
gym, or campus express a first naiveté that lacks any authority for Scripture
whatsoever. When I look at the world of my own graying and aging Gen-X
as well as the spunky, emerging Millennials, there is an absence of biblical literalism and an abundance of non-critical biblical scepticism in the
Canadian landscape. And it's not just in the world around us; it also lurks

quietly in the church. The hermeneutics of suspicion require no fertilizer in a postmodern, post-Christendom world—it grows like moss beneath humanity's feet, leaving an agnostic odor at best, and detached, cold, "country club" civil religion at its worst.

Ironically, we live in a time when we know more and less about the Bible. Today's scholars offer us wonderful tools to study Scripture, from source criticism to feminist and liberationist approaches. Yet the result has often been that people in the church feel better informed but further away from the Bible. It's like a car that was once easy to repair on our own but now needs a specialist to run fancy diagnostic tests to fix the transmission or change the oil. Kyle Small argues, "The culture of theological education, indeed the entire academy, has lost (and is attempting to recover) the ability to read a text constructively."[27]

I worry that, over time, we in the mainline churches have lost more than our biblical literacy; we've lost our trust that the Triune God can and does speak to us through Scripture. That's why I've always loved the prayer for illumination in our Reformed tradition that is shared before reading the Bible in public worship—the acknowledgment that anyone can read the Bible, but to truly understand God's wisdom, we need the help of the Holy Spirit. It's a gentle nod towards our longing for Calvin's teaching that we require the inward witness of the Holy Spirit to understand the Bible. Don't get me wrong. I love the benefits that the hermeneutics of suspicion have brought us by raising awareness of things like patriarchy in the cultures in which the Bible was written. But I worry that we have become so suspicious that we no longer live in expectation of revelation when we approach the Word of God. I don't want to send our Christian leaders out into the world Christ died to save with a TBS approach to sharing the good news. In post-Christendom Canada, our missional hermeneutics should include an equal dose of a hermeneutics of grace. Zipper pants and mesh shirts were great for the '80s, but our sovereign God, Father, Son, and Holy Spirit ,goes ahead and invites us to follow.

Years ago, a friend of mine was finishing his doctoral work and struggling with what God wanted him to do with his life. He had a hunch that teaching the Bible was part of God's plan. Not long after, in a dream, he encountered a Jesuit priest walking along the beach. The priest asked, "What

27. Small, "Missional Theology for Schools of Theology," in Van Gelder, ed., *The Missional Church and Leadership Formation*, 65. Small argues that the historical-critical method and additional methods in literary criticism have secured sacred texts for the work of destructive critique.

does God want you to do with this one life?" "Teach the Bible," came my friend's reply. "Hmm," the priest paused. "If you want to teach the Bible, first you must learn to love it."

John's Gospel makes the claim that the Bible was written so that we might believe in Jesus Christ as Lord. As a mini-library, it contains poetry, law, wisdom, history, sanctified imagination, apocalyptic vision, and much more. As missionary disciples, we hold on to Scripture as the cradle of the living Word Jesus Christ in whom we trust and believe. Reading Scripture no longer from a place of cultural hegemony, missional leaders see God's power in the Word through our human weakness. As Ellen Charry reminds those of us in the Reformed tradition, "Calvin's scriptural exegesis and his theology have the same sustained pastoral need to be threatened by a complete collapse of human strength, in order that they may learn from their weakness to depend entirely upon God alone."[28]

Why read from the Bible as a Christian community? It's not just *a* story; for us, it's *the* story. From pizza-box-filled youth rooms to stained glass sanctuaries, might we revisit the Bible with fresh eyes? Might we learn to love the Bible again, trusting it to be a faithful witness of God's revelation to humanity? Might we have ears to hear a testimony of who Jesus is for the world—yesterday, today, and forever?

Missional Catechesis

Traditionally, Christian education within Christendom meant that the broader culture participated to varying degrees in catechesis. There are many within the pews of mainline churches even today who can remember this. In other places, I've recalled my own experience of this Christendom catechesis and the profound effect it had upon me. For example, I recall my grade three teacher Ms. Duncan's final stand against secularism with Christendom catechesis. Ms. Duncan told stories of her days teaching in one-room prairie schoolhouses, still carried a ruler around the classroom for discipline, and was rumored on the playground to be 108 years old. Ms. Duncan was also a faithful member of her local Presbyterian Church. When the government rules changed, no longer permitting religion in the classroom, Ms. Duncan just went on reading Scripture every morning as she had been taught eons ago in Teacher's College (or "Normal School" as they called it). She would also begin every day by having us stand beside

28. Charry, *By The Renewing of Your Minds*, 201.

our desks and recite the Lord's Prayer. When one young budding activist (perhaps his parents were lawyers!) challenged Ms. Duncan's insistence on saying the Lord's Prayer in a public school classroom, she responded with grace and determination. "Well, class," she said in an even tone, "can anyone answer *why* we say the Lord's Prayer everyday?" Silence. Long pause. "Well, we say The Lord's Prayer day after day, until it lives inside us . . . until those words become a part of us. And one day, when you are older, and you are in trouble—you will *need* this prayer . . . you will need those words inside you. Your generation will need to work with God to make this world more like it is in heaven." I was too young at that time to know what the word "testimony" meant—but to this day I can still hear that saint testifying to her students about the power of public prayer.[29]

Ms. Duncan represented the last generation of a public school teacher who partnered with the church in a broader cultural Christendom catechesis. As the Christendom presence in the culture rapidly fades—from the Lord's Prayer in the public classroom to the Ten Commandments in the court room to the Gideon's Bible in the motel room to publically funded chaplain in the hospital room—how the church teaches and practices Christian education must also change. Now please, don't hear me in that previous sentence bemoaning this shift in society. That's the all too familiar response. No, Christian education is now properly *back* in the hands of the church where it belongs, and not tendered out to the broader culture. To long for a return to "the good old days" would force us to confront again and again the painful legacy of Christian education when Christianity in the West was yoked with political power. For us in Canada, that means revisiting such horrors as the Indigenous Residential Schools program, where we dutifully participated with the federal government in tearing First Nations children from their homes in order to westernize and Christianize them—often including unfathomable mental, physical, and sexual abuse on children as well. No, in a posture of humility, God has returned catechesis to the church and we must discover the next most faithful step.

In my teaching, I have overhauled what was formerly the "Christian education" course for our students by acknowledging that our graduates will no longer be going to large congregations with ample Christian education budgets and able, professional Christian educators on staff. Instead, the Christian education course has been retitled, "Catechesis and Community." In the class, Missional Catechesis is understood to be the process of

29. Lockhart, *Lessons from Laodicea,* 24.

transmitting the gospel in a variety of intercultural contexts, as the Christian community has received it, understands it, celebrates it, lives it, and communicates it in many ways. Catechesis, within the Christian community, educates and equips people for missionary discipleship and evangelical witness by building up the body of Christ in the world. From the Greek meaning "to echo the teaching," catechesis is understood to be a life-long process of initial call and conversion, formation, education, and ongoing conversion. Through Word, worship, service, and community, catechesis seeks to lead all God's people missionally to an ever-deepening relationship with God the Father revealed in Jesus Christ through the power of the Holy Spirit. Catechesis takes many forms and includes the initiation of adults, youth, and children as well as the intentional and systematic effort to enable all to grow in faith and discipleship through sanctification.

One of the significant shifts is acknowledging that Christian education no longer takes place on the "cradle to grave" model whereby catechesis can be based on stages of development similar to the physical body and mind growth. For example, the increasing presence of adult converts in church (and our colleges!) presents new and exciting challenges. Where do you begin catechetically when someone who has never heard the gospel presents themselves at church in their thirties or forties? It requires a missionary's skill-set like that of St. Patrick that we have not utilized in the recent past, when the culture conveyed a basic (if at times distorted) version of the gospel and we educated Christians through crèche or nursery, Sunday school, camp and youth group to adulthood. While congregations play an important role in this catechesis, my teaching now also acknowledges the other places where this important ministry takes place. Therefore, we also pay attention to what catechesis looks like in house churches, church plants and replants, and new monastic communities.

Missional Catechesis today is up front and honest about the challenges to Christian Education and seeks a way to shape, challenge, and encourage faith formation in a society that is increasingly biblically illiterate. Richard Topping notes how this shifts our way of teaching:

> A few years back I listened to an interview on CBC radio—that's the public broadcaster in Canada. The interview was with Frank Kermode, literary critic, and the interviewer began with a question like, "What is literary criticism?" Kermode responded with a short description of his subject matter—"it is the evaluation, analysis and description of literary works. We ask questions about style, form and genre, figures of speech and how an author deploys

them to achieve a literary end." The interviewer continued, "How do you teach that?" Kermode said he no longer taught criticism as such. He used to teach literary criticism, but now he teaches literature. A student can't be critical of what they haven't attended to, loved, what they have not read. Kermode, I think, like theological educators in Canada finds that the instructor cannot assume catechesis in the relevant practices and loves. The critic must become catechist first or ministerial students become articulate in their criticisms and stammer about their loves. Students have to be taught to linger with the literature, to be shaped by its moves, to let it recontextualize and master them, shock them, before they simply consume and criticize.[30]

Learning to live again as minorities in a culture unwashed in Constantinian baptismal water means acquiring an attentiveness to the need for more thorough catechesis for those who would follow Christ with their whole lives. In a sense, our post-Christendom catechesis has much in common with pre-Christendom catechesis that, according to the third-century apostolic tradition lasted for three years. In this sense, Jessica Duckworth's research on multi-year catechesis in her book *Wide Welcome* is a good example of faithful first steps towards recovering catechesis by the church. As Duckworth suggests, discipleship is learning through participation in Christian practices, "gaining knowledge and skills to sustain a Christian identity. To be clear, faith is not learned. Faith cannot be reduced to knowledge or skill. Faith is a gift of the Holy Spirit. Faith enables and sustains the life of disciples within and beyond the ecclesia crucis."[31]

Of course, catechesis is not just learning Christian practice, but practicing our faith now within a dominant culture that views the gospel on a spectrum from apathetic to hostile. Andrew Walker and Robin Parry lean into this reality when they note the early church (pre-Christendom) had to take the toxins of the pagan worldview out of converts to Christianity.

> They knew that pagan people entering the community were not coming in as blank slates ready to be written on by the Spirit but were coming in already covered in scribbles—long-term exposure to practice and beliefs that the church considered demonic. Such converts were coming already pre-formed, or de-formed,

---

30. Topping, "Troubling Context," 52.

31. Duckworth, *Wide Welcome*, 3.

from years of exposure to influences that ran counter to the subversive gospel of God.[32]

Shallow Christian faith will not survive in a post-Christendom culture. Missional catechesis provides a much-needed firm foundation of Christian identity in a post-Christendom culture where people swim in a culture of conversion based on consumerism and individualism. Like the parable of the wise and foolish builders in Matthew 7, missional catechesis provides the grounding that witnessing communities require to weather the storms of secularity. Missional catechesis longs for mature, sanctified missional disciples and knows that for faith to build that high, first we must dig deeper.[33]

Missional Pastoral Care

At first glance everything appeared normal. The Translink bus bumped along Marine Drive working its way towards the iconic Lion's Gate Bridge and that serene passage through the lush canopy of Stanley Park, before emerging in the thriving downtown of our nation's third-largest city. Beside me on the worn blue pleather seat, my son Jack (six at the time) gripped the steel bar in front of him in excitement and looked out the window as familiar sights such as play parks or restaurants on the North Shore swept by. "Look, Dad!" he said, excitement rising in his voice, pointing not outside the bus but inside at the front. Neatly positioned behind the driver was a poster for our congregation's upcoming vacation Bible school. One of our favorite soft evangelism techniques was advertising church activities on our local bus. "Look, there's the squirrel and bat and the eagle," Jack said excitedly as he named all the different animal characters who were going to whisk the large number of wide-eyed children through a five-day adventure focusing on our need to trust God. As our stop approached we grabbed the thin, frail wire and rang the bell. As we worked our way to the front something strange on the poster caught my eye. The Biblical quote at the top from Matthew 19 had been altered by a fellow passenger. It had read, "Everything is possible with God . . . " But some clever commuter had put a neat thin line in black ink through "God" and had scratched in a new philosophical statement— "Everything is Possible with pot." Nice. Only in Cascadia, I thought, as we

32. Walker and Parry, *Deep Church Rising*, 133.

33. Crofford, *Mere Ecclesiology*, 49. Crofford uses the image of a skyscraper that requires a great deal of time for builders to dig down and lay a proper foundation before the building emerges above ground.

made our way off the bus and I tried to explain in some half-baked way to my son what this new teaching was all about.

While humorous, the experience also highlighted a reality for me when it comes to pastoral care in post-Christendom. With the gospel no longer conveyed or approved by the broader culture, people have the freedom to place their trust in whomever or whatever they choose when facing a crisis. Anything is possible—whether with God or pot. Missional pastoral care begins with an awareness that the gospel is now translated into a culture where people have an overwhelming number of self-help experts and professionals to turn to when in crisis. Missional pastoral care is not a cheaper "knock-off" version of more professional counseling, rather it is theologically grounded in the essentials of the Trinitarian faith. It lives solidly within the world of theology and not psychology. Missional pastoral care is exercised through the church as a community of persons in unison with and indwelt by the Triune God. The redemptive, reconciling ministry of the Father, Son, and Holy Spirit engages the church and our pastoral ministry helps equip missionary disciples to be God's witnesses in the world.

Perhaps that's the biggest change in my practice of pastoral care when seen through a missional lens. As a pastor, I used to always think of the high point in worship as being the sermon. You work all week towards that moment. Okay, maybe that's just how a preacher sees it. But ever since missional theology seeped into my sanctified bones, I now see the benediction as the highlight of worship. God's people gathered for Word and sacrament remain critical. After all, that's how the saints are equipped for their ministry in the world. But as we turn our nametag from disciple to apostle at the end of worship, I now stand to offer the benediction and wonder, "Wow, where will God lead these people throughout the week? What conversations will they enter into that I, as their pastor, would never have in the workplace or community? Where will God lead them at home, work, or community so that they will have the opportunity to witness to Christ's faithful presence through words and works?" And then I wonder and worry, "Have I done everything I can, with the Spirit's help, to equip them for that calling? Will these people leave worship aware of the little flame above their heads?" You can see how this affects pastoral care. In Christendom, the clergy were the professional pastoral care providers. In our Reformed tradition, ruling elders were responsible for pastoral care and often did a wonderful job of caring for members in their districts. In other denominations without a strong eldership, clergy would try to train lay people in teams to do the work, but people still felt that unless you got a visit "from the pastor" it wasn't the same thing. Missional pastoral care understands that every baptized Christian has a calling to offer a pastoral presence where they live, work, and play. The pastor equips them for that witness but does not override their own ministry. In our everyday, ordinary lives we pray attention to what God is up to and open up our lives for service and witness when the time comes.

Recently, I received a text from my neighbor. We love the neighbors around us in our townhouse complex. They reflect the reality of Cascadia—bright, well-educated, kind, outdoor enthusiasts, trying to raise their kids as decent people, and all of them agnostic in their approach to Christianity. The text from my neighbor that day shared the news that her mother was dying of cancer. She knew from dinner parties, trick or treating with the kids in the neighborhood, and casual conversations that our family was Christian, or "spiritual" as many of my neighbors would phrase it. At her invitation I started meeting with the family, including the palliative woman, and accompanied them through diagnosis to death. Throughout, there was no hostility towards faith or the name of Jesus as so many believers fear when it comes to Christian witness in a secularized society. There was simply need. And trust. And longing for transcendence. In return, there was my desire to honor God through the pastoral care of a beloved neighbor.

When my neighbor's mother died, I visited the family and they asked if I could lead a memorial service. After discussing the details of the service there was a pause as I mulled over how best to offer prayer in that time and place. Before I could speak, my neighbor said, "I don't really know how to do it or how it works but I would really appreciate you praying for us right now." God's faithful presence could not have been more real in that place.

As a pastor and professor, I am mindful of the pressure of secularity upon both the church and theological education. I see it everyday. And yet, instead of leaning towards despair, I am regularly encouraged by the signs and wonders of the Holy Spirit at work around us, and within us as a Christian community. We have noted how this new post-Christendom context has changed what we teach—such as hermeneutics, catechesis, and pastoral care. But I want to close by noting that it not only changes what we teach but the teacher as well. A missional engagement with theological education, of the kind that St. Patrick desired and later developed in Ireland, shapes both the pedagogy and practice of the professor. In reflection on what this looks like for theological educators like myself in Cascadia perhaps it's best to illustrate this change by way of historical example.

Norman Bethune was born in Gravenhurst, Ontario in 1890, the son of a Presbyterian minister. He enrolled at the University of Toronto in medicine and volunteered as a stretcher-bearer in the First World War. He receieved his MD in 1916. After the War, Bethune eventually moved to Montreal where he worked at the Royal Victoria Hospital, which was the teaching hospital connected with McGill University. He published many articles and did excellent research and teaching within a traditional environment. If that was all Bethune accomplished it would be noble but not noteworthy and we would not remember him these many years later. Instead, Bethune felt called in 1936 to offer his medical skills in the Spanish Civil War on the Republican side. There in that risky and dangerous environment, Bethune began to experiment and perfect the practice of blood transfusions. His experimentation on the battlefields of Spain continued later in the field in China and helped revolutionize medicine. As a result, he is remembered today in Canada as a hero and in Spain and China as a secular saint.

In a similar way, theological education today has a "Bethune-like" quality to it. Instead of lecturing on theology from the safe confines of the seminary classroom, I see myself as a "pastor seconded to the seminary for this season of my ordained life." Teaching theological education today requires humility. It is as if one must say to the students, "I feel called to this work, I bring my pastoral experience over the years in the congregation here, but I want to come alongside you and learn at the same time. We need to practice theological reflection together as we learn what our Triune God is up to in the world."

Patrick's theological education in France prepared him for leadership within the Christian tradition but could not comprehend the mission field into which he was sent. Today, as theological educators in North America, we too need to be curious about the communities and conditions in which our graduates will be forming and nurturing Christian witnessing communities in order to best serve the *Missio Dei* in the world. Theological education in post-Christendom will require evangelical scholars who are able to equip scholarly evangelists for the mission field that is unfolding on our very doorstep.

CHAPTER FIVE

Saul

Church Planting

Hear us, most merciful God, for that part of the Church which through your servant Patrick you planted in our land.

That it may hold fast to the faith entrusted to the saints and in the end bear much fruit to eternal life: through Jesus Christ our Lord.

—CHURCH OF IRELAND'S *BOOK OF COMMON PRAYER*

AFTER RESPONDING TO GOD'S call in the "Vox Hibernia experience," Patrick leaves home despite what we can only imagine was his family's protest and tears, to set out for his training as a missionary. Prepared by a church that was more accustomed to sending priests to established parishes, Patrick is named a missionary bishop for Hibernia and returns to the land of his former captivity. Patrick is not the first Christian leader sent to Hibernia, but he will be the most effective.

It is believed that Patrick and his companions landed at the mouth of the Slaney river in 432 AD.[1] Patrick's church planting experience began

1. There is a colorful story told that Patrick and his missionary companions first landed farther south in a place called Travailahawk beach. Upon arrival, however, Patrick and company were stoned by local pagans. Apparently, one of Patrick's companions had his front teeth knocked out and was given the nickname Manntain, which means "toothless one." According to tradition the "toothless one" returned to that site years later to establish a church and give the town its name—Wicklow. As someone who has preached

here with a barn given to him for ministry by the first convert of the mission, a local chieftain named Dichu. The word for barn in Irish was *Sabhall*, from which we get the English word *Saul*. I have often wondered what Patrick said to that first convert that began his church planting ministry in Ireland. What word, what news would a pre-Christian culture need to hear that a post-Christian culture might also require today in Cascadia? As I visit with church leaders throughout the secular Northwest, I often hear different and distinctive voices in Christian communities, ranging from discouragement and disillusionment on the one end to excitement and energy for Christian witness at the other. What's the difference? Often, I've noticed it is a question of whether people have a sense of clarity around evangelistic witness and missional discipleship combined with a sense of urgency to share the gospel with others.

I had a coffee recently with a mainline pastor. She described her service with a local congregation of faithful and loving people who, year after year, continued to increase in age but shrink in number, grow in weariness, and narrow in vision. The pastor paused, tracing the rim of her coffee cup with an index finger. "To be honest, I'm at the point where I'm just trying to keep things going until I can retire," she confessed. "After that, who knows what will happen to the church." Silence. A sip of coffee. I gently explored the context of her ministry, suggesting possible missional strategies in the neighborhood and ways to build relational connections with newcomers, but the pastor seemed confused. "Well, I don't really know what I would say to a newcomer who arrived at our church. We don't really have anything to offer them," she said her voice trailing off. "You have *the gospel*," I said with a mix of pastoral sensitivity and holy frustration.

How different the conversation was that I had the following week with a church planter. Sure, this pastor wanted to talk about the challenges and frustrations of growing her new witnessing community, but there was also an abundance of enthusiasm and a joyful sense of urgency in her tone. "I love when I make a new connection in the neighborhood," she said, beaming. "I love when God gives me, or someone in our community, just the right way to translate the gospel truth into the lives of others." Her eyes lit up and she said, "We've got two adult baptisms coming up at Easter, when people are going to share their testimony about God's activity in the community. I'm thrilled about what God is doing around us and

---

in Presbyterian churches around Wicklow I realize now just how fortunate I was to get out of town with my teeth intact.

through us as a church. We've got people serving in the local community like never before and we're discovering all kinds of opportunities to name and celebrate God's faithfulness."

As I reflected on the two conversations I noted that the church planter had a sense of imperative when sharing good news with others. The church planter had a desire to build a community that included the spiritual practice of evangelistic witness and missional discipleship. The encouraging thing I've found is that this practice, this posture, of evangelistic witness and missional discipleship is in no way limited to church planting. The mainline pastor could just as easily adopt the same practice, the same posture, but too often it appears more evident in newly planted communities of faith. There is eagerness and urgency to share engaging good news.

A few years ago I was between pastoral visits and driving along the highway when my phone began to ring. Answering the phone, I instantly recognized the voice of Dylon, the children's pastor at our local church. He was breathless and half a second later it became clear that another person was on the phone line as well. Katie, another one of the youth group leaders was easily heard in the background giggling. "We've got good news!" they shouted through the car speaker, almost forcing me off the road. "We're engaged!"

And it was good news—after dating for several years this lovely couple felt God's call to take the next step of commitment. They were so excited they could hardly spit out their words. Dylon had arranged a romantic floatplane ride all over downtown Vancouver and in mid-flight fumbled in his pocket for the ring. While not altogether surprising, Katie's yes came as a tremendous relief and a source of great joy. When the plane landed, members of the youth group (playing hooky from high school with their parents' permission) were standing on the dock with champagne, ready to celebrate. How cool is that? I was honored to receive the call, delighted for them and, perhaps most importantly, amused that the next day they confessed that after speaking with me on the phone they spent the next six hours calling family and friends on the phone across the country. As Dylon said, "When you've got news this good you just can't keep it to yourself. Sure, we could have just posted a relationship status update on Facebook or tweeted our announcement, but it seemed urgent to share this good news personally with those we love."

Good news. Sharing urgent good news with those God loves seems to me to be what evangelism is all about in the wider mission of Christ's church. My love of teaching evangelism and missional leadership comes out of my devotion to the Triune God and my experience that Christ's church can be the most effective instrument of God's redeeming and reconciling mission project in this world. So let us try and establish an affirmation and clarification regarding evangelization.

The biblical roots of evangelism come from the sovereign God revealed in creation, covenant, Christ, and church as we await consummation. You'll sometimes encounter people who say dismissively, "Oh well, God is a mystery, how could anyone ever say anything definitive about God?" Well, as a Christian, it sure seems that God has gone to a lot of trouble to be made known—especially in the incarnation, life, ministry, teaching, suffering, death, resurrection, and ascension of Jesus Christ. Our God is a missional God, as the recent World Council of Churches report on Evangelism states:

> Mission begins in the heart of the Triune God and the love which binds together the Holy Trinity overflows to all humanity and creation. The missionary God who sent the Son to the world calls all God's people (John 20:21), and empowers them to be a community of hope. The church is commissioned to celebrate life, and to resist and transform all life-destroying forces, in the power of the Holy Spirit. How important it is to "receive the Holy Spirit" (John 20:22) to become living witnesses to the coming reign of God![2]

The word *evangelism* comes from a New Testament Greek word: *euangelion*. This word is a compound word made up of: "eu", meaning "good" and "angelion", meaning "message or news." It is translated into English with the word *gospel*. Walter Brueggemann reminds us that the Hebrew word *bissar* means "tell-the-news" and that this message *announced* is critical. Someone has to "say the name" but that proclamation is in light of God's action and must be followed by transformed action in the world. Brueggemann suggests interpreting evangelism in three scenes: 1) conflict between powerful forces; 2) the witness who gives testimony and tells the outcome, and 3) the listener who is invited to make an appropriate response.[3]

David Bosch contends that evangelism is that dimension and activity of the church's mission that seeks to offer every person, everywhere, a valid opportunity to be directly challenged by the gospel of explicit faith in Jesus

2. Keum, ed., World Council of Churches, *Together towards Life*, Section 2.

3. Brueggemann, *Biblical Perspectives on Evangelism*, 15–18.

Christ, with a view to embracing him as Savior, becoming a living member of his community, and being enlisted in his service of reconciliation, peace, and justice on earth.[4] As Karl Barth said,

> To address men [sic] evangelically, however, is decisively to present to them the great likeness of the declaration and explanation of the Gospel in such a way that they come to see its crucial application to them, that so far as any human word can do so it pricks their hearts that it brings them to realize that the reference is to them, or to a supremely general truth which as such demands their personal cognizance and knowledge.[5]

Now, one cannot teach evangelism in a seminary without hearing objections to the discipline, almost like you can't get through law school without hearing jokes about lawyers. One of the classic texts on evangelism, *Out of the Saltshaker,* even begins by acknowledging the awkwardness of this vital Christian practice. Rebecca Pippert confesses that there was a time where she was so turned off by the concept of evangelism that she believed "there was a part of me that secretly felt evangelism was something you shouldn't do to your dog, let alone a friend." Can you relate to this?

I begin my evangelism course by asking each student to take out a piece of paper and write down a question, "What is the gospel?" I give them a minute to answer and then they have to read out their responses. Of course, as I remind the students, how you answer the question will be based on the context of the space, community, and social location one inhabits. Nevertheless, the question is important and the answers are always interesting. I've heard quite the variety of answers over the years. While I am not looking for a uniform answer, I tell them that *how* they answer the question will affect what kind of evangelism or "good news" they share with others. In fact, their answer will determine whether or not they practice evangelism at all. When a student says, "the gospel saves us from this world so we can go to heaven," that shapes and limits what an evangelistic witness might look like when it comes to stewardship of creation, for example. When a student says, "the gospel is God's story of never giving up on humanity and the world, bringing hope and wholeness in Jesus to everything that's damaged by sin," that will shape a certain kind of faith community where healing of relationships is given priority. When a student says, "the gospel is God's prophetic word and action that

4. Bosch, *Transforming Mission,* 17.

5. Barth, *Church Dogmatics,* IV.3.2, 852–53.

unsettles the powers and principalities, declaring Jesus as Lord, converting us to Him," I know that the student will form a community over time that involves evangelism and social justice. Every now and then, when a student offers something like, "the gospel takes nice people and makes them nicer," I start considering another line of work.

I often ask my students whether there is a sense of *urgency* in their definition. Is the gospel something that requires urgent action or does it allow us to sit back and be passive? Michael Frost and Alan Hirsch identify this need for "holy urgency" as vital to churches because it creates "the right sense of immediacy to provoke holy action. It is through holy urgency that we overcome unholy complacency. When imbued with an appropriate sense of urgency, people and churches become alert and proactive, seeking information relative to development and success of their mission."[6]

What is vitally important in an evangelistic witness for church planting today is that we do not conceive of this as a "solo act" but rather as a communal action. Evangelistic witness is a group process that helps people place their trust in Jesus, and by the Spirit's power, transforms them within community into disciples of Christ who participate in God's saving mission for the world. This communal understanding of evangelization is important, as too often we have thought of evangelism as a one-person task. Karl Barth reminds us of the community's role in evangelism when he writes,

> Evangelical address as the community's ministry of witness means the inclusion of all . . . near and far, from the very first and fastidiousness even as the great sinners they are, like all members of the community. . . . It means their incorporation into the likeness of the kingdom of God which is to be offered, into the circle of the validity of the content of the Gospel and therefore of grace, of the covenant, of reconciliation, of God's humiliation accomplished for the world in Jesus Christ in order that man might be exalted.[7]

So Christian evangelistic witness is not a solo act. Just as Jesus sent his disciples out in pairs in Luke 10, so too we understand that we are participating in what the Triune God is doing in the world through the community of Christ, in the presence of the communion of saints. As Pope Francis reminds us in *Evangelii Gaudium*, local churches full of missionary disciples acting as evangelizers should never look like "someone who

---

6. Frost and Hirsch, *The Faith of Leap*, 40.

7. Barth, *Church Dogmatics*, IV.3.2, 853.

has just come back from a funeral" but rather Christian communities must recover and deepen that

> delightful and comforting joy of evangelizing, even when it is in tears that we must sow . . . And may the world of our time, which is searching, sometimes with anguish, sometimes with hope, be enabled to receive the good news not from evangelizers who are dejected, discouraged, impatient or anxious, but from ministers of the Gospel whose lives glow with fervor, who have first received the joy of Christ.[8]

I have heard some over the years question whether church planting is essentially a form of revival in the church. And, of course, in the history of Christendom, we have often seen evangelistic appeal made through revival. But revival, by its very nature, assumes a dormant Christian identity that needs to be revived, a smoldering fire that needs to be fanned back into flame. But this is increasingly not the case in a secular West. West Vancouver-based author and artist Douglas Copeland argued in *Life after God* that Generation X (born 1965 to 1980) were the first generation raised without religion in North America. Today, however, in Cascadia we have people on their second or third generation raised without religion. These are the folks who are the furthest thing from the "angry atheist" profile. Instead, they are simply affable agnostics who say things like, "Oh, so you go to church, eh? Um, I think maybe my Grandparents did that. That's nice, I'm off to run on the seawall in Stanley Park or ski down the North Shore mountains this morning."

No, church planting is not about revival but like Patrick landing in Ireland and forming his first Christian community at Saul, it is making evangelistic witness—good news as new news a core principle. Patrick himself writes about the importance of this evangelistic witness in his Confession.

> It is right that we should fish well and diligently, as the Lord directs and teaches when he says: "Follow me, and I will may you fishers of men." And again he says through the prophets: "Behold, I send many fishers and hunters, says God"; and other such sayings. Therefore it is very right that we should cast our nets, so that a great multitude and crowd will be taken for God. Also that there should be clerics to baptise and encourage a people in need and want. This is what the Lord says in the gospel: he warns and teaches in these words: "Go therefore and teach all nations, baptising them in the

8. Pope Francis, *Evangelii Gaudium*, 10.

name of the Father and of the Son and of the Holy Spirit, teaching them to observe all that I have commanded you; and behold I am with you all days, even to the end of the age."[9]

What makes Patrick's evangelistic witness all the more remarkable is that it was out of step with the dominant church culture of his day. Just as many mainline Protestants struggle with the concept of evangelism, let alone engaging in evangelistic conversations with coworkers or neighbors, the Roman Empire of Patrick's time was not a culture that placed a great emphasis on evangelization. By Patrick's time people in the Roman towns and cities had been largely converted to Christianity, but rural people were more or less cut off from the proclamation of the gospel and were still pagan. As Maire de Paor argues,

> Individual bishops of the caliber of Irenaeus of Lyons in the second century, and Martin of Tours and Victricius, Archbishop of Rouen, in the fourth, made all-out, individual efforts to rectify this situation. But, with one exception, there was seemingly no organized, concerted effort made to go out and convert pagans, beyond the confines of the Western Roman Empire, until the Benedictine Pope, Gregory the Great, initiated it, in the person of Augustine of Canterbury, in the dying years of the sixth century. Patrick's mission to the Irish pagans was that exception.[10]

For a minority now in the majority secular culture, evangelistic witness must also be accompanied by missional discipleship. The bumper sticker for missional theology has become "the church doesn't have a mission, rather God's mission has a church." It has always puzzled me that while the sovereign God could accomplish it alone, the Triune God invites us as sinful and fallible creatures to come alongside and participate in mission with that simple invitation, "Come and follow me." The church is the instrument of God's mission in the world as we live out our part in God's eschatological plan for creation's redemption. But too often mission and evangelism have been synonymous in the church and there *is* value in making a distinction between the two concepts. Mission, according to David Bosch, is the wider of the two terms and involves the

> total task that God has set the church for the salvation of the world. In its missionary involvement, the church steps out of itself,

9. Patrick, *Confession*, Section 40.

10. de Paor, *Patrick the Pilgrim Apostle of Ireland*, 23.

into the wider world. It crosses all kinds of frontiers and barriers: geographical, social, political, ethnic, cultural, religious, ideological. Into all these areas the church-in-mission carries the message of God's salvation. Ultimately, then, mission means being involved in the redemption of the universe and the glorification of God.[11]

Michael Goheen notes the distinction between *mission* and *missions* when he writes, "*Mission* is the vocation to embody God's renewing work before the nations across the breadth of human life. *Missions* is the activity of establishing a witnessing presence in places and among peoples where there is currently no Christian presence."[12]

In the last twenty years the language of "missional" has exploded in popularity and thus, decreasing in clarity leading to everything from "missional beekeeping" to "missional cooking." Therefore, it is important to define what we mean by this term. By *missional*, I mean that the essential vocation of the church is to be God's called and sent people in the world, trusting that God's mission has a church.[13] Recognizing that a hard and fast definition of "missional church" is elusive, it is possible to say missional leaders seek an alternative imagination for being the church in the world, where God's Spirit is at work transforming us as a community through mystery, memory, and mission.[14] With a deep trust in the witness of the Triune God, missional discipleship recognizes that God's being and doing are one, and since God's actions always flow from who God is as Father, Son, and Holy Spirit, so too should the church seek to unify its being and doing.[15] Missional theology understands that the Triune God's mission is to restore the world through the healing of the nations.

Missional disciples take seriously the Triune God's active presence in the world, playing out in God's story of redemption between Christ and consummation. Missional disciples are trained to exegete both the

11. Bosch, "Evangelism," in Chilcote, ed., *The Study of Evangelism*, 9.

12. Goheen, ed., *Reading the Bible Missionally*, 24–25. Goheen builds his argument upon Lesslie Newbigin's distinction between a "missional dimension" for all of life and a "missional intention" for specific elements of life.

13. Guder, ed., *Missional Church*, 11. Rooting it in a deep witness to the Triune God, Guder defines missional ecclesiology as biblical, historical, contextual, eschatological, and possible for all disciples to practice.

14. Roxburgh and Boren, *Introducing the Missional Church*, 45.

15. Sparks et al., *The New Parish*, 81. As the Parish Collective argues, "Mission cannot be conceived as a project of the church, rather, the church exists within God's reconciling mission."

Scriptures and the communities God calls them to serve. This dual focus on text and context, gospel and culture, is important given the shifting sands of ministry within our North American landscape and especially here on the West Coast and throughout Cascadia.

In order to have an effective evangelistic witness, Christians in this post-Christendom context need to have a solid theological grounding as a minority voice in their workplaces, schools, recreation centers, city halls, and community forums. Too often we have tried to offer our witness from the strength and power position of the majority in Christendom. Today, we are learning that evangelization often takes place over time and is grounded in firm relationships, requiring both holy speaking and holy listening. Canadian missiologist Lee Beach argues, "Listening is the evangelistic act of genuine presence and authentic relationship that mirrors the incarnational activity of Christ and is the essence of mission."[16] This kind of humble, holy listening and holy speaking is discernible in the ministry of the first bishop of Armagh. Patrick, landing on the shores of Ireland to proclaim the gospel, did not have the benefit of power and prestige and in that sense was more like the New Testament church planters. Consider the bold and remarkable claims made by a minority group of Christians like this:

> But you are a chosen people, a royal priesthood, a holy nation, God's special possession, that you may declare the praises of him who called you out of darkness into his wonderful light. Once you were not a people, but now you are the people of God; once you had not received mercy, but now you have received mercy. Dear friends, I urge you, as foreigners and exiles, to abstain from sinful desires, which wage war against your soul. Live such good lives among the pagans that, though they accuse you of doing wrong, they may see your good deeds and glorify God on the day he visits us.[17]

Note how the New Testament does not consider this evangelistic witness and missionary discipleship as reviving lapsed cultural Christianity. No, there is clarity that as a minority group, "strangers and pilgrims" as the King James Version puts it so nicely, our evangelistic witness is tied to the quality

---

16. Beach, *The Church in Exile*, 209. Beach goes further and says, "Listening is not simply a pre-evangelistic act of relationship building, not something that we must do in order to gain credibility so that we can get to the real business of telling people what we know they need to hear. We listen in order to hear people's stories, to understand their lives, to identify God is already at work and to discern signs of spiritual hunger. Listening is the place where authentic relationship is forged."

17. 1 Peter 2:9–12, *NIV.*

of our relationships with one another in the Christian community and our neighbors outside. As one scholar noted regarding Patrick's missional leadership, evangelization was, "God-with-us, transforming minds and hearts by the grace and love which constitute His presencing to us. Supremely active for Christ, St. Patrick nevertheless saw spiritual development as a growing from within, mind and heart being the medium of faith—life with Christ whose God-filled humanity is for us and of our salvation."[18]

Our missional discipleship involves spiritual development that traces its sanctified steps back to our covenantal status with God in baptism. This is not a calling reserved for the religious professionals, there is no "outsourcing of baptismal vows to paid clergy" in this form of Christian witness. No, it is an acknowledgement that our gathered life together as a Christian community is for the purpose of our scattered life to live in the community as, foreigners and exiles, with the calling of evangelistic witness and missional discipleship. By seeing the world through a doxological lens we live, speak and, act differently than those around us.

Through my study and practice of missional theology in Cascadia, for example, I have noticed a curious shift in my own focus of Sunday worship, as noted in the previous chapter. While appreciating the gathering of God's people in worship, as well as the building up of God's people through Word and sacrament, I undervalued the "sending" of these equipped saints into the world. My work with Darrell Guder at the Centre for Missional Leadership has helped me focus on the importance of what flows from worship. Often, I would close Sunday gatherings in the past with the words like, "Our worship ends so that our service may begin." While true, it is not just service but *witness* that flows out of our worship of the Triune God. While I still deeply value the gathering of God's people in worship, the act of confession; the beauty of community prayer; the singing of spiritual songs; the reading and preaching of God's Word; the feasting around the Lord's Supper; the sacrificial offering of God's people and the affirmation of the Apostle's Creed; I now pay particular attending to the blessing and commissioning. As mentioned earlier, when I stand at the front of any church I am amazed and mindful that the eclectic group of missionary disciples before me will soon be sent out into the community to bear witness to the gospel of our Lord Jesus Christ. *Their words. Their actions.* Not mine. The people before me at the end of worship will have access to others that I will never have access to—in their homes, on the

18. Conneely, *St. Patrick's Letters*, 216.

bus, at work or beside the soccer pitch. What will they say? What will they do? Will God's reputation in Christ be enhanced or diminished? Jeff Greenman notes this critical step of worship by saying

> In theological terms, it is important that congregants do not merely leave the service—they are commissioned. People do not wander away on their own to do whatever they wish but are sent out with a clear purpose. In Christian tradition, the element of dismissal at the end of worship has a rich meaning. The Latin derivation of the word "dismissal" comes from "mission," which refers to our being "sent out" as God's people into God's world to do God's work.[19]

This benediction as call to witness is essential in a post-Christendom context like Cascadia, where the gospel is "new news" to so many who have been raised without awareness of Christ's resurrection. Again, in post-Christendom we turn to Patrick in a pre-Christian context with curiosity and eagerness to learn.

When I think about that conversation between Patrick and his first convert, Dichu the Chieftan, I want to listen in and hear how Patrick witnessed to the gospel. I've heard Adam Hamilton at Church of the Resurrection suggest that Christians need to struggle with and discern answers to questions like, "why do people need Jesus, why do people need church, why do you need *this* church?" Patrick had to make a clear and conscious communication about why people in Hibernia needed Jesus and the specific expression of Christian community Patrick was building. How did Patrick describe Jesus as Lord and Savior to that first convert? What did he say about a Christian fellowship that moved Dichu to provide space for the ministry? What did Patrick say to those in days afterwards that convicted them of their need for Christian community, forgiveness of sins, study of the Word, and participation in communion with God through the sacraments?

For too long, Christendom leadership has assumed a common starting place with those who are not Christians since the culture conveyed a distorted but minimal understanding of the meaning of the gospel. Today, however, pre-Christendom church planting and post-Christendom church planting have something in common—telling an old, old story that sounds new to people's ears. I was reminded of this while travelling along in a funeral hearse and chatting with a kind-hearted, agnostic funeral director in Cascadia. He asked a question that took me by surprise. "Ross, what's so good about Good Friday?" It was the middle of Holy Week. And as most

19. Greenman, *Pedagogy of Praise*, 84.

clergy will tell you, the relationship you build with the local funeral director is unique—one part professional and the other playful. This particular funeral director and I shared a similar sense of humor. In fact, he claimed working together helped put the "fun" back in funerals. That's why his serious question from an agnostic-leaning-toward-atheist colleague on the way to a graveside committal took me by surprise.

"What's so good about Good Friday?" Before I could collect my thoughts, the director added, "We do good work together, but I doubt most families would call the day they bury their loved ones 'good.' So why is the church's biggest funeral of the year—for Jesus—called good?" The budding trees whipped past the window as we continued down the road, their blur of new life giving me time to think. *Good. Friday.*

"Well, I've always been a bit puzzled by that too," I said. "From what I've read, the etymology of the phrase is kind of fuzzy. Some people think 'Good Friday' evolved from 'God's Friday,' just like 'goodbye' evolved from 'God be with you.' The 'goodness' of Jesus' grappling with sin and death on the cross was more a witness of humble holiness than a hoarse-voiced hallelujah."

"Yeah, but what does it mean *for you?*" the director asked pointedly. I mulled over this deeper question as I watched a couple of vehicles pull to the side, respectfully allowing our funeral hearse to carry on down the highway. My mind drifted to one of my favorite sermons from John Wesley, that scholarly evangelist ancestor in the Methodist tradition. Recalling his arguments in the 1760 sermon "The New Birth," I said, "I suppose the goodness of Good Friday for me is the definitive statement that what God has done in Jesus is *for* us. God risked being in relationship with humankind knowing that rejection was always possible. The pain, betrayal and rejection on Good Friday is awful, but the Trinity is revealed in that moment as being *for* us and not against us. That awful day was the critical turning point in the story of God's redemption of the whole world."

I paused for a moment, watching the director nod in agreement. "As Christians," I said, "or at least as people trying to figure out what it means to follow Jesus, we know that the 'good' in Good Friday lies in what God has done *for* us. But that's only half of it. Jesus said to a conversation partner named Nicodemus on a moonlit night, 'You have to be born again; you have to be born of the water *and* the Spirit.' The goodness of Good Friday is only complete when we experience not just what God has done *for* us, but what God does *in us* through the new birth of the Holy Spirit." I saw the director subtly raise an eyebrow at that comment. I continued, "Call it what you will—new birth, born again, Spirit-washed—but the goodness of Good Friday is complete when we know and trust both what God has done for us in Jesus and *in* us by the Holy Spirit." The director chewed on this awhile as we whipped along the highway.

"So, if that's true, then why don't I see more Spirit-filled folks in the church?" he asked flatly. Ouch. Returning to Wesley's witness, I said, "Well, maybe we've got a whole lot of church people who are born of the water but not of the Spirit. You know, the folks who think the church exists to take nice people and make them nicer. John Wesley had a phrase for folks like that: 'the almost Christians.'"

The funeral coach turned off the highway and drove through the cemetery, a long line of cars behind us giving the appearance of a black snake winding its way through the grass. I reached for my Bible and the director for his vial of sand, the two of us assuming our roles again for the sake of the grieving family. As I stepped outside, I wondered, in the week the church calls holy, whether we might lean once more toward that Friday, trusting that on the cross we encounter a God whose Son is *for* us, and in an empty tomb a God whose Spirit is at work *in* us. If God were to see us leaning, loving, and living into that new birth, might God bless that new creation, the body of Christ, broken yet beautiful, with the same affirmation as that first day long ago, by calling it good?

That rich and honest conversation with a funeral director reminded me how people in a post-Christian culture are open to the gospel, but what a responsibility we have to be "clarifiers of tradition" alongside witnesses to the resurrection. Sometimes the biggest stumbling block to our post-Christendom witness is the baggage of our Christian heritage or the frail and woeful (at times hypocritical) witness of the church visible all around us. A response to the anemic witness from the established church for many in this post-Christendom era is to engage in sowing seeds or planting fresh expressions of new worshipping, working, and witnessing communities of Christian faith. If this is the calling or recalling for us in Cascadia as the new fruit of our election by God's grace, then we must be careful not to repeat the errors of our Christendom past. Church planting in a post-Christendom context requires a prayerfully discerned vision—an ability to see what others cannot see.

I was reminded of that while visiting San Francisco with my wife and some friends. Our little group stood outside an art deco building in the downtown core that, at first glance, looked no different than any other in the trendy, hipster neighbourhood. We checked in at the front desk and with our shiny visitor ID badges were hustled into an express elevator to the top floor. The doors opened and before us whirled a sea of intelligent humanity— Twitter world headquarters. #Overwhelmed. The friends we were travelling with had a cousin who, at the time, was the chief legal counsel for Twitter. He greeted us and showed us around the open concept workplace—no private desks or even pen or paper. Employees simply showed up and found a creative space. A gourmet kitchen was set in the middle of the office—chefs standing by to fuel that entrepreneurial spirit through culinary magic! Everyone working there appeared to be twelve years old and a genius like Doogie Howser, M.D. It was amazing to witness all this from a start-up company that began in 2006 and changed the world of communication in 140 characters. Over lunch on the rooftop patio, I asked some of the employees about the success of the company that has grown to almost 300 million users worldwide. One bright young man, who probably picked up his doctorate from MIT before getting his driver's license, offered an opinion. "Most people think that entrepreneurs need to be risk takers," he said in an earnest voice, "but it's more than that." He paused for effect and leaned in close as if to share a secret. "Being an entrepreneur today requires one to have vision to see what others cannot see."

Our post–Christendom state means that Gen Xers and Millennials (those veterans working for Twitter!), not only lack any social pressure to be involved in a Christian community, but also have no Christian memory. I wonder what might it mean to be more entrepreneurial in the sharing of the good news? I returned to the Twitter wisdom, "One must have vision to see what others cannot see." It reminded me of John 11, where Lazarus dies before Jesus can reach him. Martha scolds Jesus for being late and reminds him that if the Lord had hustled, her brother would still be alive. Martha was about to learn, however, the truth that God may not show up when you want—but God's always right on time.

Jesus arrives late, weeps with those who are weeping, but then does something no one expected. Jesus sees something the others do not see. "Take away the stone," the Lord commands. "No way!" comes the response. "He's dead and there's a stink." Undaunted, Jesus models some missional discipleship—seeing life where others see only death. "Lazarus, come out!" Jesus says and the world is reminded once again that the strange rhythms of God's grace can turn any dying into a rising. Many look at the mainline

Protestant churches today and see only death. We desperately need leaders who can see life where others speak only of decay. I would love to discover how God might be glorified if we could flip the script from focusing on death to declaring boldly, "Take off the grave clothes and let the church go!"

Church planting in Cascadia not only requires an appreciation for evangelistic witness but a solid commitment to missional discipleship. This is so different from the Christendom legacy, where one was asked by the church for little more than participation in Sunday worship and offering—or as I call it, "noses and nickels." Instead, new witnessing communities are holding people to a higher standard. We are called to recognize our identity and responsibility as that royal priesthood the Bible speaks of in 1 Peter 2. Priests are, by their very nature, a minority of the population but they serve the community through making intercessory prayer and sacrifice to God. What sacrifice might we be willing to ask of missionary disciples in post-Christendom?

A couple of blocks from my home on the beautiful North Shore of Vancouver is the helicopter pad for the all-volunteer North Shore Rescue Organization. North Shore Rescue consists of approximately forty volunteers skilled in search and rescue operations in mountain, canyon, and urban settings. They are open to everyone on the North Shore if they meet the following criteria: "If you are fit, know the local mountains, and are interesting in making a difference in your community, consider applying to volunteer with North Shore Rescue." Recently, the community fundraised for a new building to house the North Shore Rescue and their equipment. It's a beautiful new space compared to their old, cramped quarters of the city public works yard. But no one thinks that the North Shore Rescue is about the building. It is simply a place of equipping. The mission of the North Shore Rescue is clear and on the lips of most North Shore residents. If somebody gets lost up the mountain, the volunteers of the North Shore Rescue team spring into action to save a life. Imagine, however, if now with their brand new building the North Shore Rescue started admitting members to the team who liked the time of socializing and education at the new and improved location but had absolutely no interest in going up the mountain to rescue someone in trouble. How long until the mission and purpose of the team was weakened to a state of disaster? Now think about the church, a place of equipping its members to participate in God's ongoing mission of salvation in the world, of reconciling and healing for the nations. How might our existing Christian communities or the new church plants popping up in Cascadia make clear that the purpose of belonging is that we are saved to serve God and neighbor? No armchair disciples here. No, the benediction of our equipping worship is where we turn our nametag from disciple over to apostle and we are sent out to be Christ's witnesses where we live, work, and play. Every time I hear the helicopter lift off near my house on the North Shore I am reminded that Christians are called to a life-saving work of our own here in Cascadia and around the world.

As Jeff Greenman argues about Christians,

> We are people whose purpose is being together is God-centered. We are not a social club of people who choose one another's company for the sake of mutual enjoyment. We are not strangers to one another randomly collected as at a bus stop, but the body of Christ, those who belong to each other in a more profound way than any social club can offer. Our social, economic, racial and ethnic identities are secondary to our primary identity as God's people. Being rich or poor, healthy or sick, young or old, white or black, and so on, do not form the basis for our gathering, nor the core of our personal identity.[20]

Church planters that I spend time with in Cascadia are aware of the challenges of Christian witness today, but they are also relentlessly open to the movement of the Holy Spirit in this place. Recently, I visited and preached in three different church plants that my students are leading in Vancouver and Victoria. All three offered evidence of a sensitivity to the agnostic funeral director's questions about faith, the twitter employee's epiphany-like invitation to see what others do not see, and the North Shore's Rescue organization's high standards for community participation.

My first visit was to St. Peter's Fireside in downtown Vancouver, a church plant, equipped through Tim Keller's Redeemer City-to-City Network ministry, that meets in the University of British Columbia's Robson Square campus. A former student at our college and friend, Roger Revell, serves as pastor of discipleship to the church plant and organizes small group ministry in condos throughout the downtown core of Vancouver. The worship style is an "ancient-future" blend of Anglican liturgy and evangelical worship style. In worship they practice what I would call a "teaching liturgy," where they take time to say why they do what they do in worship. I first learned this style of worship while on exchange with the Presbyterian Church in Ireland, serving Kirkpatrick Memorial Church in the

20. Greenman, *Pedagogy of Praise*, 24–25.

Ballyhackamore neighbourhood of Belfast. In the early 2000s Kirkpatrick was down to its last few members and was set to close. The congregation petitioned the Presbytery for one last call. With permission given, they called a Regent College graduate who arrived with his family and set about building a missional ministry team that over a decade partnered with the Holy Spirit in a revival ministry. By the time I arrived on exchange for the summer, they were worshipping with pews full and a congregation made up of all stages and ages of life. In worship I noticed the community's commitment to a teaching liturgy. Every week they would use a part of the liturgy in simple and powerful ways to communicate the gospel. Instead of simply beginning a prayer of confession, a worship leader might say, "How's your week been? Did you do everything right? Did you make mistakes? Is there a conversation or email you wish you could take back? Are you ready to be honest about your brokenness, your sinfulness that separates you from God and other people? Let's pray about it . . ." St. Peter's Fireside has a similar approach, not a "seeker-sensitive" format from the 1990s but a way of equipping the saints (and sinners!) while worshiping the Triune God. St. Peter's Fireside has witnessed great gains in the so-called "secular downtown" of Vancouver. Their small group ministries include a weekly gathering over a meal in a host's condo. After dinner and prayer, they explore a different theme each week that can take the group "upward"—Bible study and focus on communion with the Triune God—and "inward"—confession of sin and prayer requests shared without judgement or fixing from small group members, as well as "outward"—a monthly mission outreach program in which each small group makes a commitment to building relationships with those in need. Expectations are high for those who would join this witnessing community. While hospitality at St. Pete's is a priority and sincerely offered to newcomers, this is not a Christian community for bystanders. St. Peter's Fireside is having a real impact on downtown Vancouver as a church planting community.

Another visit was to St. Andy's Community Table, a student-led, faculty-supervised church plant in the West Point Grey neighborhood of Vancouver. Student missional leaders Andrea Perrett and Andrew Devanbu share their leadership role with others in the community, inviting community members to share their gifts with others. Meeting on Sunday evenings in a local Presbyterian church hall, St. Andy's Table is a "RePlanting" initiative of the Centre for Missional Leadership at St. Andrew's Hall. RePlanting as a branch of church planting seeks to establish new witnessing Christian

SAUL

communities in congregations that have died or are in their final life cycle. For mainline Protestants RePlanting is important since often these denominations today are property-asset rich yet missional-skill-set poor.

St. Andy's Community Table meets Sunday evenings in the West Point Grey Presbyterian Church, beginning with a delicious meal and an invitation to sit down with friends and strangers engaging discussion questions crafted with the evening's Bible story in mind. For example, on the night I visited the biblical focus was part of a Seven Deadly Sin series and the text was Matthew 25:14-30: the parable of the Talents. In order to "prime the pump" for the reading and preaching of God's Word, exploring the sin of sloth, people shared a meal and asked each questions like:

What is your favorite excuse for not doing something?

Would you rather stay in your pajamas all day (but have to leave the house in them) or wear your daytime clothes (but have to sleep in them)?

Describe your ideal lazy day.

What is one chore that you always try to get out of doing?

In the parable the Master says, "Well done good and faithful servant"—What would you hope to hear from God when you meet God face-to-face?

How have you noticed/discovered God at work in the world this week?

At least a quarter of the community gathered are children and while they participate in the discussions at the table, many also play in the corner, coloring and racing toy cars. After dinner, a host for the evening invites responses to the questions. With worship songs and Scripture printed on the place mats, others lead singing on guitar and piano. Then someone reads the Bible lesson of the night. A different preacher each week offers a five- to ten-minute reflection or "sermonette." The children are encouraged to engage in the teaching time while enjoying a fruit popsicle. Prayer and the doxology conclude the evening and then everyone pitches in to clean up the space. A special effort is made to challenge people on their "sentness," in other words, how their week and witness will be impacted in light of the evening's reading. For those who are free, a group wanders down the street to the local coffee shop or pub for more conversation on the biblical story. The St. Andy's Table experiment, meeting in the hall of a historic 1912 church building,

65

is an example of Christians today seeking to form vibrant community as a minority group in the ruins of Christendom.

Another vivid example of this movement of the Holy Spirit was on a recent trip to Victoria, the capital city of British Columbia. At the turn of the last century and the height of whatever Christendom power existed in Cascadia, Victoria was of equal size to its neighboring city across the water—Vancouver. Today, however, Victoria has a population of 86,000 (365,000 in the Greater Victoria region) while Vancouver has ballooned to a population of 630,000 (2.5 million in the Greater Vancouver region). As a result, Victoria appears today to have a large number of church buildings in this small city and yet records even greater numbers of residents with "no religion" than Vancouver in the census data. It was interesting, therefore, to visit and speak with the people of the Abbey church plant that meets in the Fernwood Community Centre located across the street from a large nineteenth-century Baptist church building that is now used as a performing arts space. My former students, now ordained Anglican priests, Meaghan and Rob Crosby-Shearer, lead this new church plant that again blends traditional Anglican liturgy with evangelical worship style and music. Children are invited to come forward in the beginning of the service setting up their "altar" in front of the main rough-hewn communion table by placing a small box full of sand and setting up a simple cross, placing a lit candle (battery operated!) and an icon of Jesus. Worship is participatory with members of the community leading prayers and praise. On the day I visited prayers were offered first by the community by writing down prayer concerns and weaving the strips of paper onto the wall. Weekly Eucharist grounds the community in the experience of Word and sacrament and their participation in the local community is highlighted by way of invitation for others to join them in projects of justice and mercy.

All three of these Cascadian church plants are small by "church growth model" standards but they are faithful in the context that they find themselves in. Christian witness and missional discipleship through church planting cannot be measured by the old Christendom legacy of "noses and nickels." No, instead there is an understanding that evangelistic witness and missional discipleship form the heart of the community quite apart from church growth. Church planting in a post-Christendom context is a minority act of faithfulness to the sovereign Christ that understands more fully what the Bible means when it "seasons and shines" a fallen and redeemed world by salt and light, illuminates hope as a city on a hill, lives bravely as sheep among wolves. Reggie McNeal predicts an "explosion of missional communities" in the years to come. But he cautions that church planting will look very different then when we had a bricks-and-mortar understanding of what church meant. It will more like church planting in the New Testament when church did not mean buildings or budgets. McNeal suggests future churches planted will "range in size from a handful of participants to a few dozen. Gatherings will take place in homes and restaurants, bookstores and bars, office conference rooms and university dorm rooms, hotel meeting areas and downtown Ys, and yes, even churches."[21] He imagines the common life of these missional communities centered on an intense desire for spiritual growth and maturity alongside the deep desire to bless the neighbourhood where they live, work, and play.

McNeal's forecast for the church sounds a lot like Patrick's past witness as the mission in Ireland began not in a bookstore or bar but a barn. Patrick would need to be attentive to the spiritual growth of his mission community and its wider impact as he landed back in Ireland and planted his first church in Saul. Now the gospel would be preached beyond the reach of the Roman Empire. Where the Pax Romana had failed in Hibernia, the Pax Christi was ready to move and transform lives. Imagine the scene: Patrick and his assistants worshipping the Triune God in a little barn on a windswept hill, living out a story of God's relentless pursuit of humanity and creation that cost God his Son's life. You can still visit that windswept hill where Patrick first planted his church. I return there with my own children every time I visit Ireland. A few miles outside of Downpatrick, on a little back road sits Saul Church. Built by the Church of Ireland for the fifteen-hundredth anniversary of Patrick's arrival and opened on All Saint's Day in 1933, the tiny, beautiful stone chapel sits open and alone, inviting people to pause and pray. The barn, long gone of course, would still look appropriate where the church now sits—the backdrop a cascade of rolling green hills as far as the eye can see. A simple black and white sign proclaims, "On the site of this Church St. Patrick built the First Christian Church in Ireland 432 AD. Here is the most ancient ecclesiastical site in this land, the cradle of Irish Christianity." As one kneels at the railing, gazing up at the beautiful stained glass window of the shepherd slave turned Saint, it is clear that while every church planter may not be remembered 1,500 years later, each and every plant is a new birth, a cradle of Christianity, proclaiming the goodness of God and the truth of the gospel to a sinsick and beloved world.

21. McNeal, *Missional Renaissance,* 179.

CHAPTER SIX

Slane

Confronting the Powers

It is impossible for us to have the gospel without affliction.

—JOHN CALVIN

AS A FREQUENT GUEST preacher in Cascadia, I can often tell a congregation
that is struggling with life beyond Christendom. One of the telltale signs is
when the pastor or a senior lay person points out to me who the "important"
people are in that church. Sometimes it comes in an excited whisper while
singing hymns at the front of the church. Often the awkward moment comes
with great flair while, shaking hands at the door of the church, the minister's
voice leaps like a gazelle when introducing the parishioner stressing their
socially significant role for others around to hear. Perhaps it is during the
low point of the liturgy for introverts—coffee hour—when people cluster
in groups and interact with others something akin to a junior high school
dance. Whatever the context, it will be clearly pointed out to me who the
"important" people are in the church—so and so is the CEO or CFO of this
or that company; here is the former mayor of the city or a perhaps a lawyer
or judge; this person or that is a member of this political or power broker
group. *Jesus wept.* I try not to roll my eyes but what I hear behind the statement is "we're still important as the church because we're connected to the
powers." But the reality of exile in post-Christendom is that these desperate
attempts to stay connected to the power of this world sounds more like Ron
Burgundy in *Anchorman*: "I don't know how to put this but I'm kind of a

big deal. People know me. I'm very important. I have many leather-bound books and my apartment smells of rich mahogany."

For a church with an identity tied up in Christendom and longing to be "a big deal," the idea of being the people of God in conflict with the dominant culture is strange, foreign, and scary. But as Lesslie Newbigin reminds us, "Ministerial leadership for a missionary congregation will require that the minister is directly engaged in the warfare of the kingdom against the powers which usurp the kingship."[1]

For Patrick, arrival back on the shores of Hibernia came with the assumption that he was engaged in spiritual warfare, "not against flesh and blood, but against the rulers, against the authorities, against the powers of this dark world and against the spiritual forces of evil in the heavenly realms."[2] After establishing his first base where Saul Church now resides in County Down, Northern Ireland in 432 AD, Patrick engaged the powers and principalities of Ireland in order to convert them to Christ.

One of the most famous encounters took place at the Hill of Slane on Easter in 433 AD. At Tara, the political center of the Kingdom of King Laeghaire, Patrick defied the Druid law and lit the Easter fire on the Hill of Slane, today in County Meath, not far from Dublin. Tara was both "the pre-eminent centre of royal power, to which noblemen in dispute would come for judgment, even from as far away as the far northwest of Connacht, and an ancient site which could not be detached from its pagan past."[3] Perhaps time softened Patrick's memory as he summarized the conversion of the Irish from pagan Druid practice this way: "How wonderful it is that here in Ireland a people who never had any knowledge of God—who until now have worshipped idols and impure things—have recently become a people of the Lord and are now called children of God."[4]

Others, however, have been more than pleased to recount through markedly more colorful tales of the confrontation between Patrick and the spiritual and political powers of the land, slipping into the murky world between history and hagiography. Visiting the Hill of Slane today, you encounter a windswept hill with a stoic statue of Patrick staring towards the hill of Tara and the center of power in his day. Leading pilgrimage tours to this site, I invite people to imagine Patrick lighting the paschal

---

1. Newbigin, *The Gospel in a Pluralistic Society*, 240.

2. Eph 6:12, *NIV*.

3. Charles-Edwards, *St. Patrick and the Landscape of Early Christian Ireland*, 20.

4. Patrick, *Confession*, Section 41.

fire on Easter Eve to celebrate the resurrection of Jesus Christ, the light
of the world. I invite people to look over at the Hill of Tara and imagine a
group of Druid priests livid at Patrick's Easter flame. This simple action of
faith by Patrick brought with it the penalty of death as the Druid's "state-
anctioned" law said that on that holy night fires should be extinguished,
with the exception of lighted by the priests in Tara alone. Patrick sought
to hijack this pagan practice by lighting a huge fire on the Hill of Slane. I
invite pilgrims to imagine the king and his warriors making their way to
the Hill of Slane on their chariots. For tradition states that upon seeing
Patrick's fire King Laeghaire asked who it was that had violated his law. As
Jonathan Rogers reminds us,

> Ireland had no central government. Instead, it had a hundred or
> more petty kings, each ruling a tuatha, or tribe. This tuatha might
> be as small as a few hundred people, or it might include thousands,
> but it was very much a local unit. An individual's rights were pro-
> tected within his or her tuatha; outside the tuatha, however, there
> were no guarantees. Only three classes of people were guaranteed
> safe passage from one tuatha to another: kings, priest and poets.[5]

Patrick was clearly neither a king, Druid priest, or poet. He was
travelling the Island without any earthly protection and now he was in
trouble. The Druids, supported by the various kings or chieftains, carried
with them the Celtic culture's folklore and served as arbitrators of justice.
They conveyed the folk religion of the land to the people with goddesses
ruling in the natural world and gods in human arts and institutions.[6] As
Philip Freeman states:

> The inhabitants of ancient Ireland worshipped many gods and
> goddesses, each with particular areas of expertise, much like those
> of the Greeks and Romans. The god Lug, known across Celtic
> Europe, was a divinity of many skills who was honoured at his
> festival of Lugnasad in early August. Other gods included the
> paternal Dagda, his son Oengus, and Ogma the patron of poets.
> Among the many goddesses were numbered Danu, the divine
> mother, the beautiful Fann and Li Ban, and Brigid, a goddess of
> wisdom and prophecy who shares many qualities with the later
> saint of the same name. The priests of the Irish were the druids,
> who had also been present in Britain and continental Europe. The

5. Rogers, *St. Patrick*, 20.
6. Ibid., 21.

druids included in their many skills the performance of sacrifice and prophecy.[7]

But Patrick lived in a different story. He lived within the world of the gospel and his lighting of the paschal fire on Easter Eve was his statement of Christian faith in the land where the Druids held power. The Druids warned the king that if Patrick's fire on the Hill of Slane were not put out before morning, it would never be extinguished, and that the man who had set the first in defiance of the king's orders would be exalted above kings and princes.

The High King of Tara was furious at this proclamation and set out by chariot with his soldiers to kill the one who set the fire on Slane. When Laeghaire came in sight of Patrick and his companions, he was warned by the Druid priests not to go near the fire but to send for the saint, and orders were given that no one should harm the man until the king spoke to him.

The tradition records that as Patrick approached the King he sang Psalm 20:7, "Some trust in chariots, and some in horses; but we will call on the name of the Lord our God." Patrick eventually confronted the Druid priests under the leadership of a man named Lochru. It didn't end well for Lochru. As Muirchu's *Life of St. Patrick* recalls the encounter, at the words of Patrick, "the druid was lifted up into the air and fell down again, splitting open his skull on a rock. He died in front of everyone, and the pagans were afraid."[8] The story continues as Patrick and his missionary disciples escape the king only to reappear the next day at Tara and challenge the Druids in a show of divinely-inspired force that included the elements of nature with fire and ice. Legend has it that Patrick managed to perform many feats and miracles to prove to the king that the Christian God was far more powerful than the old gods, and he used a three-leafed shamrock to explain the mysteries of Christianity to the King. The contest of power demonstrated the authority of Patrick's God and the High King, while not converted to Christianity, allowed Patrick to minister in his lands.

It's hard not to hear the Old Testament echo of Elijah facing the prophets of Ba'al at Mount Carmel in this traditional story of Patrick versus the Druids. Elijah held a special place in the imagination of the early church and in Patrick's *Confession* he tells a story of being afflicted by the devil and calling on the name of Elijah to defend himself. Patrick's Elijah-like confrontation between God's servant and pagan priests, watched closely by

7. Freeman, *The World of Saint Patrick*, 4.

8. Ibid., 73.

a human king with power to bless or harm the ministry of the prophet, is a story of courage and faithfulness of biblical proportions.

Of the various churches that I visit in Cascadia I find the formerly mainline churches appear to struggle the most with this call to confront the powers and principalities. It's ironic since these denominations often self-identify as social justice supporting churches, but have done so traditionally from a position of strength and coziness with power. For some, there is simply blindness to the ways in which the gospel has been reduced and the church domesticated by Western values of consumerism and individualism. As the Parish Collective in Seattle warns

> Economics functions as a mirror, where the truth about your faith is reflected back. The spreadsheet is a theological statement, reflecting any incongruence between what you say you believe and how you steward your resources. This reality can be painful. The close connection of economics to the practicing of your faith is reflected in the simple principle that Jesus communicated: "Where your treasure is, there your heart will be also. . . ." To think of faith and economics primarily in terms of philanthropic giving is to fundamentally mistake what economics are and why they are so powerful. At a core level economics has to do with basic exchange, receiving and giving. This exchange is behind common word pairings such as spending and earning, investing and accruing, or borrowing and lending. The connection between your treasure and your heart is not simply about how you give; it's also about how you earn, which means there is nothing that has to do with money that doesn't have to do with your heart. Your heart is connected to your treasure.[9]

For others, looking away from our immediate captivity to idols of wealth and power to the more recent Christendom past is painfully informative. For example, in Canada, the mainline church enjoyed partnership with power dating back over centuries since the founding of New France and the British Colonies in places like Nova Scotia and Upper Canada. This alliance with state power has had long-term, damaging effects on God's reputation. For example, as mentioned in a previous chapter, the mainline churches' partnership with the federal government in state-sponsored, church-run residential schools for Indigenous people tore children away from their families, degraded their culture in favor of Western ways and often subjected them to verbal, physical and

9. Sparks et al., *New Parish*, 97–98.

sexual abuse has humbled once great Christian communities.[10] My own denomination's apology included these words:

> In our cultural arrogance we have been blind to the ways in which our own understanding of the Gospel has been cultur- ally conditioned, and because of our insensitivity to aboriginal cultures, we have demanded more of aboriginal peoples than the gospel requires, and have thus misrepresented Jesus Christ who loves all peoples with compassionate, suffering love that all may come to God through him. For the church's presumption we ask forgiveness.[11]

More recently, the Truth and Reconciliation Commission has demon- strated the danger of what happens when the church aligns itself too closely with power. Crisscrossing Canada, members of the Commission heard painful testimony from survivors of the residential schools and is- sued a report that included a "Call to Action" for all Canadians as well as specific guidelines for Christians, such as, "We call upon church parties to the Settlement Agreement to develop ongoing education strategies to ensure that their respective congregations learn about their church's role in colonization, the history and legacy of residential schools, and why apologies . . . were necessary."[12]

Sadly, the response to the fallout from residential schools has too of- ten been missional paralysis rather than a deeper alignment with the risen Christ's activity in a world not yet brought to consummation by grace. Karl Barth picks up on this danger when he cautions against a "strange neutral- ity" in any time or place when a clear articulation of the gospel against the culture is called for, concluding:

---

10. As mentioned earlier, as with all critiques of Christendom, we must be careful not to give the impression of a deist reading of history whereby God is thought to be "absent without leave" from creation, church, and community for 1,500 years. Rather, like Bon- hoeffer in Nazi Germany, we are beginning to identify prophetic Christian witness in the midst of corporate sin, including residential schools. Addressing the one hundred-forty- third General Assembly of the Presbyterian Church in Canada, Cindy Blackstock, the head of the First Nations Child and Family Caring Society of Canada, praised the work of Dr. Peter Bryce, a chief medical officer and member of St. Andrew's Presbyterian Church Ottawa, who spoke out against the care of Indigenous children in residential schools and was silenced and sidelined as a result.

11. Apology to First Nations from the one hundred-twentieth General Assembly of the Presbyterian Church in Canada.

12. Truth and Reconciliation Canada, *Honouring the Truth, Reconciling for the Fu- ture*, 330.

that it regards its Lord as One who is absent in a past and future distance, so that it is superfluous to listen for His living Word here and now, and pointless to attest it to the world? Are we not challenged by the alarming question whether in this relation to Him it does not betray far too close a resemblance to the priests of Baal on Carmel?. . . In virtue of its proclamation of a general, timeless, neutral and blunted instead of concrete truth, it might still claim and even to some degree enjoy a certain validity in the eyes of men as one of the constructs and forces of world-occurrence. In this way it might make it easier for the world to recognize and tolerate if not to accept itself and its function. For what particular objection can the world have to a church which understand and discharges its task in so innocuous a way?[13]

Where is there evidence of sin, evil and brokenness in our context that prevents human flourishing? Where are we called as witnesses to the resurrection, as ambassadors of Christ, as agents of reconciliation to speak up and speak out against the powers and principalities at work in Cascadia and beyond?

Ministering in the ruins of Christendom reframes our role as missionary disciples primarily in terms of witness. Like Patrick lighting a paschal fire to declare Jesus Christ as light of the world, we are called as individuals and as communities to stand out and to speak up as those who have placed their trust in the risen Christ. Darrell Guder argues

The term *witness* integrates the who, the what and the how of Christian mission. The Christian individual is defined as Christ's witness; the entire community is defined as a witnessing community; its impact upon the world into which it is sent is observable witness; all its activities are, in some way, a form of witness— demonstration of the gracious rule of the Risen Lord. God's Spirit, working in mysterious and gracious ways, empowers this very human and very fallible witness to be the means by which people hear the good news and are invited to become followers of Jesus. The purpose of incarnational witness is "so that grace, as it extends to more and more people, may increase thanksgiving to the glory of God."[14]

For the formerly mainline church, acknowledging, let alone engaging, in the reality of spiritual warfare is awkward and unseemly, something

13. Barth, *Church Dogmatics*, IV.3.2, 816.
14. Guder, *The Incarnation and the Church's Witness*, 6.

"those other churches" taught about. If we are to lean into missional lessons from St. Patrick in his pre-Christian context for the sake of ministry in our post-Christian context, however, we must understand ourselves to be, at times, on a twenty-first-Century Hill of Slane. It was deliciously ironic, therefore, when I recently encountered a mainline musician who objected to including the following verse in worship from the great Celtic Hymn "Be Thou My Vision":

> Be Thou my breastplate, my sword for the fight;
> Be Thou my Dignity, Thou my Delight;
> Thou my soul's Shelter, Thou my high Tower:
> Raise Thou me heavenward, O Power of my power.

"I don't like the violent imagery and the people at our church would be offended by it," the musician said in a tone that reeked of dismissive superiority. I replied that the members of your affluent congregation feel no tension whatsoever with singing the verse, "Riches I heed not, nor vain earthly praise, thou mine inheritance, through all my days." Huffed the musician, "Well, I don't know about that. I just like the tune and don't want to be offended by the lyrics." I responded, "And what is the tune name?" Fumbling with the hymnbook, the musician answered, "Slane." I offered, "Let me share a little story about what happened on the Hill of Slane . . ."

Missional leadership in a post-Christendom context acknowledges that the world is not as safe as we used to believe when we were living in a Constantinian, baptized society. Living as a minority in a larger culture that is dominated by late-stage capitalism, nation-states, and a secular ethic of pursuit of self-advantage over communal care, missionary disciples are wary of the battleground for truth and justice. We are engaged, for this season of the church's life, in an eschatological struggle against forces that would do us harm. True minority Christians, living in places like Egypt, Iraq and Pakistan have much to teach us about the reality of living and preaching the gospel against the powers and principalities of this world. Colleagues from those contexts that I meet would have no trouble singing about the breastplate of righteousness and sword of the Spirit required as a minority in a hostile context.[15] Neither would they deny that the struggle ends in God's victory as they sing

15. Eph 6.

High King of Heaven, when the battle is done,

grant Heaven's joy to me, O bright Heaven's Sun!

Heart of my own heart, whatever befall,

Still be my Vision, O Ruler of all.

Therefore, Patrick's example of faithful Christian witness in the midst of conflict empowers us as missionary disciples today in post-Christendom to nurture and equip witnessing communities to proclaim Jesus Christ, crucified and risen, in the midst of principalities and powers that would do us harm. Patrick continued his ministry after Tara, expanding his circle of influence throughout the Island and enhancing the Triune God's reputation with each most faithful step. Even now, so many years later, Patrick is remembered for his grace-filled leadership of moving people from darkness into the light of Christ. As The Church of Ireland prays,

Almighty God,

in you providence you chose your servant Patrick

to be the apostle of the Irish people,

to bring those who were wandering in darkness and error

to the true light and knowledge of your Word:

Grant that walking in that light

we may come at last to the light of everlasting life;

through Jesus Christ our Lord.[16]

16. Collect for St. Patrick's Day, *The Book of Common Prayer, The Church of Ireland*, 305.

CHAPTER SEVEN

Cashel

Conversion

When we tell the story of our own conversion, I would have it done with great sorrow, remembering what we used to be, and with great joy and gratitude, remembering how little we deserve these things.

—CHARLES SPURGEON

COURAGEOUSLY FACING OPPOSITION TO his missional discipleship, Patrick continued to move around the Island of Hibernia bearing witness to the resurrection of Jesus and offering a call to conversion to Christ. One of those places Patrick visited became a visible symbol of Patrick's evangelizing ministry—Cashel. Tradition states that St. Patrick visited Cashel to meet, teach, and baptize the powerful king of Munster, Aonghus. While some have seen Patrick's missional approach of befriending the local chieftains as a way of aligning the gospel with the equivalent of "state power," the reality, as noted earlier, is that given the social convention of the day he could not travel from one territory to another without the permission of the local king or chief. Therefore, his relational evangelism with kings was essential in order to spread the gospel through the Island of Hibernia. Of course, as an evangelistic witness to the gospel, looking to convert pagans to missionary discipleship, he would also preach the gospel and pray for the Holy Spirit to move people's hearts. And every now and then it worked! Indeed, the conversion and baptism by the king of Munster attracted a great crowd and proved influential in Patrick's ongoing ministry.

Patrick officiated at the baptism but at the end of the worship service, likely carried away with his preaching, he accidentally thrust his bishop's staff or crozier through the foot of King Aonghus, who didn't even flinch. Of course, all the spectators were shocked at this action towards the king. At the conclusion of the baptismal service, the king stood and limped away. Servants rushed in and dropped to their feet to bind the wounds of the king. When Patrick realized what had happened, he apologized to those gathered there and took Aonghus aside to ask why he did not say anything when the accident happened. The King calmly replied, "Oh, I just thought that was part of the ritual." Despite this rocky start, it was the beginning of Christianity on the Rock of Cashel.

It's encouraging to know that St. Patrick made mistakes, but it is even more edifying to know that he continued his focus on clear proclamation of the gospel, despite the dangers present in a pre-Christian culture. This focus should give us direction and encouragement in our own post-Christian context. As a more recent missionary, Lesslie Newbigin, stated, "I cannot doubt that the call to conversion is essential to any authentic understanding of the gospel."[1] Patrick faced the daunting challenge of evangelizing a pre-Christian culture and offering a call to conversion and the Sacrament of baptism. Baptism in Patrick's context was a serious commitment, as many Roman Christians delayed baptism, "sometimes until the last possible moment," since practical wisdom became "sow one's wild oats, and then have the whole slate cleared by baptism—a practice which effectively destroyed the sacramental life of Christians."[2] Patrick's preaching to pre-Christians with his call for conversion to Christ through baptism meant giving up a former way of life and "putting on Christ" for a whole new worldview. For Christian leaders today, we live in the ruins of Christendom but the call to conversion and baptism into life with Christ is no less daunting than it was for Patrick. For us, the signs of Christendom's crash are all around us. While there are many beautiful examples of the Holy Spirit's power at work in growing congregations, often overwhelmingly made up of newcomers to Canada, other churches are clearly struggling. In "Euro-stock" mainline denominations in particular, many congregations are graying and declining. While headlines in other parts of the West include angry atheists who make believers feel foolish for their faith, in Cascadia many are not angry with Christianity but simply apathetic towards the church. Tina

1. Newbigin, *The Gospel in a Pluralistic Society*, 239.
2. O'Loughlin, *Saint Patrick*, 22–23.

Block's research concludes that churches have not struggled due to strong criticism or unbelief but what she calls "comfortable indifference," stating that "religious indifference seems to have been especially comfortable in the Pacific Northwest."[3] Indeed, I would describe the good-natured people I bump into as "non-practicing agnostics." As Patrick made his way to places like Cashel to preach the gospel, we too should look around our context and ask, given the culture of the day, why would anyone choose to become a Christian? How is Jesus' message still relevant in this secular age where, according to Canadian Philosopher Charles Taylor,

> The buffered identity of the disciplined individual moves in a constructed social space, where instrumental rationality is a key value, and time is pervasively secular. All of this makes up what I want to call "the immanent frame". There remains to add just one background idea: that this frame constitutes a "natural" order, to be contrasted with a supernatural one, an "immanent" world over against a possible "transcendent" one.[4]

What might conversion look and sound like in a world now where the "immanent frame" of the horizontal plane trump cards talk of a transcendent or vertical plane? The end of Christendom brings this reality to the fore. In *Why Christian?*, Canadian theologian Douglas Hall confesses, "The Christendom into which I was born . . . no longer exists—pockets and vestiges of it notwithstanding. Few people in the Western world today are 'caused' to be Christians by the sheer accident of birth. Many may start out that way, but fewer and fewer find inherited Christianity reason enough to stay Christian."[5] Now, some may be totally discouraged by this state of affairs, especially if they grew up in a Canada where "inherited Christianity" was the norm and where being a good Christian and a good citizen went hand in hand. Any Generation X or Millennial pastor is likely to hear about those "glory days" while visiting with older Christian adults. "Reverend, I remember when there were 1,000 children in the Sunday school and we had to set up special classrooms in the janitor's closet just to fit everyone in." Funny thing, however, is that those of us in leadership from younger generations don't remember those days. We recall Sunday school as sitting with a few other kids in a mold-infested, crumbling 1950s-era Christian education wing with a faded blue-eyed and blond-haired Christ poster in

---

3. Block, *Secular Northwest*, 63.

4. Taylor, *A Secular Age*, 542.

5. Hall, *Why Christian?*, 14.

the corner, aimlessly doodling on connect-the-dot Jesus coloring sheets to keep us busy. The glory days of Christendom are simply not part of our memory, and that may be a huge advantage in the years ahead.

Instead of trying to get back to the glory days, God invites us to look forward in hope, trusting that just as the Almighty went ahead of the people like a pillar of cloud by day and a pillar of fire by night, so too our Triune God is moving forward—the holy ground ahead of us saturated with pre-venient grace. I'm excited about the "refiner's fire" that God is putting the Western church through at this time because it forces us to make a deci-sion between an emphasis on institutional survival and partnering with the Lord to help make disciples for Jesus. To those in the mainline church in Cascadia and beyond who cling to "the good old days," Jesus speaks a clear word, "Those who want to save their life will lose it, and those who lose their life for my sake, and for the sake of the gospel, will save it."[6] Christian leaders in a post-Christendom context ask themselves and their witnessing communities, "What is God calling us to give up or die to in order to find our life in Christ and experience human flourishing?" Questions like this force us to reexamine concepts like evangelism and conversion that our Christendom past has turned away from, when most were born "nominally Christian." St. Patrick's missionary discipleship helps us catch a glimpse of what witness looks like when following the Jesus of Palestine rather than the Jesus of Constantine.

For many who have been raised in a church where the language of mission, evangelism, and conversion were thought unseemly, this can cre-ate anxiety. The reality, however, is that as human beings in the West we simply swim in a culture of conversion. A consumerist culture that strives every minute to convert you from Pepsi to Coke, from Gap to Calvin Klein and from Cialis to Viagra is anything but benign. As Bryan Stone reminds us in *Evangelism After Christendom*, in "every direction we turn, we are offered the promise of 'makeover,' whether of body, face, wardrobe, career, marriage, home, personality, or soul."[7]

In such a context, we need to find an effective witness to "the hope within us."[8] Why become a Christian today? What might we say to the "Kings and Queens of Munster" in our neighborhood, on the soccer pitch, in the coffee shop, around the workplace or at the yoga studio? Recognizing

6. Mark 8:35, *NIV.*

7. Stone, *Evangelism After Christendom*, 258.

8. 1 Peter 3:15, *NIV.*

that everyone in the world is navigating their way through life using some sort of philosophical map and compass, how do we articulate and live out an example of the extravagant, life-changing love and grace of Jesus Christ that has reoriented our lives? While there are many philosophical paths and religious influences that beckon in this world, surely the vision and promise we've glimpsed in the Father, Son, and Holy Spirit is so unbelievably compelling that we will continue as missionary disciples to make a case for why becoming a Christian matters. The invitation to experience real life with the Trinity, to see our lives as created and blessed by the Almighty, to follow a path that's narrow with a love that's wide, is an intoxicating and totally consuming way of life. To follow Jesus, to rest in his assurance, to wrestle with his teaching, to put in practice gospel medicine in a sinsick world, is at the same time wonderful and painful, challenging and encouraging, personal and global.

Of course, ultimately we don't choose to be Christian at all; Christ chooses us. Cultural Christianity set the bar so low for discipleship with its "nickels and noses" membership requirements of "show up and put up" that we are now in a season of witness that can create Christian community to be low barrier but high expectation. Following Jesus does not promise a burden-free life, prosperity by the world's standards or ten easy steps to a better you. No, as my colleague and friend Jason Byassee is fond of saying, "All God's gifts to us are cross-shaped." German pastor and martyr Dietrich Bonhoeffer's witness proclaims that truth all too clearly and yet it was Bonhoeffer himself who said in *The Cost of Discipleship* that simply, "Discipleship means Joy."

As we noted earlier from Tina Block, a curious reality of Christian witness in post-Christendom Cascadia is that those aligned with Christ are not battling angry atheists at every turn. Oh yes, there are those kind of folks around and it is a helpful reminder of the end of our privileged Christendom legacy to be mocked and derided for our faith in Jesus. It just happened to me recently in a conversation in the neighborhood. It is curious, however, how strongly some atheists feel the need to *evangelize* Christians about their *unbelief* but when Christians talk about God in public it's somehow offensive and unseemly. Sure, at times we find ourselves on the Hill of Slane or Tara like Patrick, engaged with powers of unbelief. But more often in the ruins of Christendom we find ourselves like Patrick at Cashel, having to engage in basic apologetics, to lean into a teaching ministry that takes catechesis seriously and follows the Holy

Spirit's movement towards conversion and baptism with adult converts. E. A. Thompson suggests that Patrick, like Augustine of Canterbury, offered a witness of works and works, holy speech and holy living whereby "they gave themselves up to unbroken prayer, watching and fasting. They preached to all whom they could button-hole."[9]

This is an encouraging word to those who now understand themselves as Christians to be a minority in society and wonder how best to live. Instead of encountering angry atheists all the time, ministry in a post-Christendom context has Christians mixing often with affable agnostics. These are people for whom participation in a Christian witnessing community may seem as foreign and antiquated as renting a DVD or, heaven forbid, a VHS from a pic-a-flik store down the street.

Christian witness in a post-Christendom context relies exclusively on the movement of the Holy Spirit to disrupt people's "map and compasses" in order to open them to the life-giving presence of Jesus Christ. This is a transforming act of the Holy Spirit that converts people from one way of experiencing and understanding the world to another. As John Calvin once wrote concerning the conversion of Saul to Paul in Acts 9, "The beginning of conversion is such that God without having been called or sought, by His own initiative seeks us who are wandering and going astray; that He changes the inflexible desires of our heart, so that He may keep us open to His teaching."[10]

God changes the *inflexible desires of our heart*, so that he may keep us open to his teaching and have a heart to witness to the gospel and serve our neighbor in love. What a beautiful way to describe what takes place in our conversion to Christ and baptism into a new way of life. God's call comes to those whom God chooses at a particular time and place. Now, we may say, "Hey, I'm not that bad a person. I'm not an ISIS terrorist. I pay my taxes and give what I can to charity. I'm trying to be a nice Canadian or a friendly American." Again, we return to Calvin, who said, "All do not rise up against the Gospel with such great violence as Saul, but both pride and rebellion against God are nevertheless innate in all; we are all by nature perverse and cruel." As a teenager, when I accepted Christ and responded with gratitude to God's grace it was a clear choice. The world said—deep down we're basically good people. The gospel said—deep down we're selfish, sinful, messed up and in need of God's rescue and forgiveness. When I weighed those two

9. Thompson, *Who Was St. Patrick?*, 90.

10. Torrance, eds., *Calvin's Commentaries*, Acts 9.

options it became clear that only one of them was true. God's call leads to conversion. As Darrell Guder argues,

> There is in late Western modernity, a continuing resistance to the blunt biblical message of human sinfulness. But if the good news of God's love in Christ is to transform us, God must confront our profound need for transformation and challenge us to repent. The possibility of conversion, as God's continuing work in us, is the core of the good news. It demonstrates the faithfulness of God as the one whose gracious action in Christ can really make us into new people, can initiate a new creation.[11]

God's call leads to a real and noticeable change in our lives. I sometimes wonder if the problem with our churches is that there isn't enough evidence around of God's transformation od us. Is there evidence that we've been changed by the power of the Holy Spirit?

I sat recently on a Saturday locked up in a church basement interviewing dozens of young adults looking for a position at our Presbytery's summer camp. Only camp interviews could include back-to-back questions like, "Who is Jesus Christ?" and "Are you okay with shaving cream and water balloon fights?" What impressed me most was the ability of the teens to articulate the call of God in their lives. The most interesting question, however, is not "tell me about your call" but "describe the kind of God that would call you to discipleship."

For example, there is no doubt that there is something dramatic happening in the classic call story of Saul on the Damascus road in Acts 9. The Bible says that Saul was blinded by his encounter with the resurrected Lord Jesus and led into Damascus where he did not eat or drink for three days. God's call leads to conversion. But that's only part of the story. Then the Bible speaks of a disciple named Ananias in Damascus. I think this is possibly the best and most overlooked part of the whole chapter:

> In Damascus there was a disciple named Ananias. The Lord called to him in a vision, "Ananias!" "Yes, Lord," he answered. The Lord told him, "Go to the house of Judas on Straight Street and ask for a man from Tarsus named Saul, for he is praying. In a vision he has seen a man named Ananias come and place his hands on him to restore his sight." "Lord," Ananias answered, "I have heard many reports about this man and all the harm he has done to your holy people in Jerusalem. And he has come here with authority from

---

11. Guder, *The Incarnation and the Church's Witness*, 15.

the chief priests to arrest all who call on your name." But the Lord said to Ananias, "Go! This man is my chosen instrument to proclaim my name to the Gentiles and their kings and to the people of Israel. I will show him how much he must suffer for my name." Then Ananias went to the house and entered it. Placing his hands on Saul, he said, "Brother Saul, the Lord—Jesus, who appeared to you on the road as you were coming here—has sent me so that you may see again and be filled with the Holy Spirit." Immediately, something like scales fell from Saul's eyes, and he could see again. He got up and was baptized, and after taking some food, he regained his strength.[12]

Calvin makes a fascinating observation on this passage. Is it not strange that Jesus, the Lord of all, addresses Saul—the great enemy of the church—and blinds him on the road to Damascus only to turn him over to a third-rate disciple named Ananias? Okay, well, Calvin doesn't exactly say that—but close. In other words, why would Christ in his sovereignty call a fallible, fragile human being to instruct Paul in this critical moment—on his way to becoming the greatest evangelist of the early church? Ananias hears the call but is worried, given Saul's reputation. But Christ ministers through him to reach Saul turned Paul. As Calvin writes, "For if Christ subjected Paul to the instruction of a common disciple, who are we to be reluctant to hear any teacher, provided he has been ordained by Christ, in other words, proves himself in actual fact to be His minister?"[13]

This humbling act leads Paul into the church through baptism. This story from Acts 9 is often shared in church as the call or conversion of St. Paul, but it is also a story about Ananias—it's a story about us, the church, and our role in God's ongoing story of salvation in the world, whether pre-Christian or post-Christian. Like Patrick at Cashel, God continues to gather his people, build them up through Word and sacrament in order to send them out into the world to serve as witnesses to the resurrecting and reconciling power of the Triune God. The story of Ananias is reassuring in that we are not left on our own to engage in ministry but rather, like John the Baptist pointing to Jesus, we witness to the gospel that transforms lives. Eugene Peterson captures something of his when he reminds us that the pastor does not simply tell the story of Jesus but rather, "he or she merely affirms the fact that there is a story to be told, and goes on to provide the opportunity and stimulus for persons to construct and tell

12. Acts 9: 10–19, *NIV.*

13. Torrance, eds., *Calvin's Commentaries*, Acts 9.

their own stories as personal and local instances of the story of covenant faithfulness."[14] James Torrance offers us a helpful reminder that our evangelization that leads to baptism is actually a way that helps us understand what it means to be truly human beings:

> To hold out Jesus Christ to the world is not only to hold our personal salvation and eternal life in our evangelism, but it is also to give all people their humanity. Whatever else the incarnation means, it is that all people and all races—Jew or Gentile, black or white, male or female—are meant to see their humanity assumed by Christ, sanctified by his life in the Spirit of unbroken communion with the Father, by his death and resurrection, offered to the Father "without spot or wrinkle," and given back to them in the mission of the church.[15]

In the ruins of Christendom, the Triune God is on the move calling and converting human beings to follow Christ and participate in the life of Father, Son, and Holy Spirit. As missionary disciples witnessing to this truth we have a front row seat to witness the Holy Spirit turning people away from crass materialism and the empty values of this current age toward a relationship with the living God we know in Jesus Christ. There is a price, of course, but it is worth it.

Years ago a husband and wife joined in regular worship at our congregation. Neither of them were Christians, but through some Christian friends and the hospitality of the local church, they started worshipping week by week. They asked a million questions, attended our Christianity 101 course, and started to engage in the disciplines of following Jesus. After a year they asked if they could be baptized in Sunday worship. I was thrilled, as were the elders of the church. A few days before the baptism Sunday they came to meet with me in the church office. We engaged in a little small talk but I sensed they had come to ask a specific question. Eventually they got around to their real purpose of the visit. "My wife and I were just wondering, um, how much does it cost to be baptized?" I was caught off guard and taken a little aback. I didn't think very long about their question and assumed they meant, "is there a fee for baptism?" I stammered, "Oh it doesn't cost anything, it's God's grace, it's free." They seemed pleased and after a few more minutes of chat they left to continue their day.

14. Peterson, *Five Smooth Stones for Pastoral Work*, 90.
15. Torrance, *Worship, Community and the Triune God of Grace*, 104.

As soon as they left my office, I knew that I had made a mistake. I wanted to call after them but they were already out of the building. I sat back down at my desk and looked at the text for Sunday's service:

> When Jesus saw the crowd around him, he gave orders to cross to the other side of the lake. Then a teacher of the law came to him and said, "Teacher, I will follow you wherever you go." Jesus replied, "Foxes have dens and birds have nests, but the Son of Man has no place to lay his head." Another disciple said to him, "Lord, first let me go and bury my father." But Jesus told him, "Follow me, and let the dead bury their own dead."[16]

That Sunday as we celebrated the baptism of these two adult converts to Christianity, people who were engaged by missionary disciples in the community, welcomed to "belong before they believed" within the worshipping life of the church, and who encountered the risen Christ through his broken yet beloved body. I spoke about the cost of discipleship. I apologized for giving the answer that "it costs nothing to follow Jesus." I was wrong. I told the congregation that, in fact, it costs *everything*—our whole lives. By turning our whole lives over to Christ, however, we participate in the abundant life of the Son of God in this world—a victory achieved long before we were ever asked to give our "yes" to God's grace-filled invitation to discipleship. This was a little like Karl Barth's famous answer to the question when was he was saved: "I was saved 2,000 years ago on a hill outside Jerusalem named Calvary." In the end, following Jesus costs everything since it cost the Son of God his life. It's a high price. But the price is right.[17]

---

16. Matt 8:18–22, *NIV.*
17. Lockhart, *Lessons from Laodicea,* 154.

CHAPTER EIGHT

Armagh

Missional Ecclesiology

"The problem is not that the church is institutional
but how it is institutional."

—DARRELL GUDER

PATRICK RECEIVED FREE PASSAGE and support for his evangelistic witness throughout Hibernia by befriending local chieftains at a minimum, and converting them to Christ at best. As Patrick moved from region to region preaching the gospel, baptizing converts, and ordaining leadership, he faced the challenge of how to organize his mission with an ecclesiology and polity that would be theologically in line with Rome but nimble enough for the mission field.

Patrick established the headquarters of his mission in what is now known as Armagh, in the north of Ireland.[1] Patrick selected the location based on its close proximity to Eamhain Macha, known today as Navan Fort, the capital of Ulster and home to a "high king" or powerful chieftain. Kings or chiefs were like our North American mayors today. While they may have the same title, the mayor of Vancouver or Portland is seen as having more influence and power than the Mayor of Bellingham or Kamloops. The "mayor" or high king of Ulster was understood in Hibernia to be on par with Tara in Meath or Cashel in Munster. Archaeologists date human

---

1. O'Loughlin, *Saint Patrick*, 9. Armagh is considered the traditional headquarters of Patrick's ministry. Some debate this claim and certainly the see of Armagh worked hard to assert this claim through the promotion of Patrick's connection to the area most clearly through the eighth-century *Book of Armagh*.

settlement at Eamhain Macha as far back as 6,000 years ago, during the Neolithic period. It is believed that by the time Patrick arrived, the settlement had moved to slightly higher ground (away from the site of Navan Fort that you can visit these days, complete with actors dressed up as "pre-Patrick" pagans) closer to the downtown of Armagh City today. From the higher ground they continued to dedicate the space to their pagan goddess Macha and called it "Macha's high ground" or Ard Macha, which easily became *Armagh* over time. The *Annals of the Four Masters* remembers Armagh's beginning and purpose this way:

> Ard Mhacha was founded by Saint Patrick, it having been granted to him by Daire, son of Finnchadh, son of Eoghan, son of Niallan. Twelve men were appointed by him for building the town. He ordered them, in the first place, to erect an archbishop's city there, and a church for monks, for nuns, and for the other orders in general, for he perceived that it would be the head and chief of the churches of Ireland in general.[2]

Armagh remains the "ecclesiastical capital of Ireland" for both the Roman Catholic Church and the Anglican Church of Ireland, even though Armagh itself is a small city of only 15,000 people, dwarfed by the larger and more important cities of Dublin, Belfast, and Derry. In Patrick's day, however, it was a strategic choice. Close to the seat of political power, due west about seventy miles from Saul Church where Patrick began his ministry, Armagh proved to be an ideal site for the administration of the growing church in Hibernia. It is believed that the structure of Patrick's Irish church followed his relational evangelism with chiefs in the local tuaths. As David Dumville notes, a traditional form of "ecclesiastical government was established on Irish soil as Christianity came to be made secure in its second generation. The primary unit of social and political organization was the tuath, to which the diocese was therefore adapted. The number of bishops started to increase accordingly."[3]

The basis of society was the extended family—the tribal unit known as the tuath. Alannah Hopkin says of the tuath community, "They lived in isolated farmsteads defended by a ditch and bank system encircling the dwelling houses. The remains of these ring forts (raths) can be seen today all over Ireland."[4] Patrick was able to adapt ecclesiastical structures to the

2. O'Donovan, *Annals*, 64.

3. Dumville, *St. Patrick*, 180.

4. Hopkin, *The Living Legend of St. Patrick*, 20. The buildings within the raths were

new realities he faced in Ireland. As Ludwig Bieler notes, "In adapting the organization of the Roman Church to the conditions of Ireland, where there were no cities, he seems to have made the tuatha (states) his dioceses; the episcopal sees, called civitates, were probably organized on a quasi-monastic pattern. Being himself a lover of monasticism, he transmitted this love to the Irish."[5]

While we have some clarity how Patrick practiced his evangelistic ministry in Ireland and built alliances with local chiefs, the actual structure of the young Irish church is a little less clear. There is a document entitled, "The First Synod of Saint Patrick" that includes all kinds of "rules and regulations" for church conduct and administration such as "Alms from pagans shall not be accepted by the church" and "If any priest has built a church, he may not offer mass there until the bishop consecrates it, as a right," as well as some more odd ordinances like "any clergyman . . . who is seen without a tunic and does not cover the shame of his belly and his nakedness or if he has not cut his hair in the Roman manner or if his wife has gone about with her hair unveiled, then let them be held in contempt by the laity and excommunicated from the church."[6] Along with the "no shirt, no shoes, no service" regulations the First Synod of St. Patrick also enforced a "Billy Graham/Mike Pence" rule of not being alone with a member of the opposite gender: "A monk and a virgin—he from one place and she from another—shall not stay together in the same guest house, nor shall they travel from one town to another in the same vehicle, nor shall they carry on long conversations."[7] While the thirty-four rules of the First Synod of Saint Patrick offer evidence of structure for the early Irish Church, scholars are clear that the document is dated after the death of Patrick and is more a reflection of the church that grew out of his ministry rather than the structure he developed in the mid-fourth century.

Studying Patrick's evolving ministry and ecclesiastical structures gives us an opportunity to reflect on our own challenges and opportunities regarding polity and governance for a post-Christendom missional church. The Euro-stock churches that emerged out of the Reformation have a

---

simple, thatched structures with little to offer in the way of comfort. Each tuath consisted of a hierarchical aristocratic community that lived under the protection of its ruler the ri (king) or taoiseach (chief).

5. Bieler, *The Works of St. Patrick*, 7.

6. Freeman, *The World of Saint Patrick*, 39.

7. Ibid.

dismal track record of Christian unity while building their ecclesiastical frameworks. The late nineteenth- and early twentieth-century ecumenical movement that grew, in part, from the practical realities of the mission field (either abroad or in the western regions of Canada and America) proved to be an ecclesiastical band-aid solution that lost its adhesiveness over time. I teach my students in Presbyterian church history about how Canadian Presbyterians imported to Canada all the bitter arguments from the "old country" regarding the Free Church movement and the Church of Scotland. The Methodists, of course, did the same thing with Wesleyan Methodists and Episcopal Methodists and so forth. While the Presbyterians managed to get their act together in 1875 and form one national church, and the Methodists did the same thing in 1884, soon the march towards church union and the creation of the United Church of Canada in 1925 would tear families and communities apart, leaving the Continuing Presbyterian Church and new United Church clergy, congregations and colleges with bad blood for years to follow. Church historian Phyllis Airhart illustrates this Christian ill will through the personal writings of the author of the best selling series *Anne of Green Gables*.

> The day after the inauguration of the United Church of Canada, author Lucy Maud Montgomery mulled dejectedly over glowing newspaper accounts of its "birth." In recent years she and her husband, Ewan Macdonald, a Presbyterian minister, had made no secret of their opposition to the proposed union. Nevertheless, one of his two pastoral charges had voted to unite with the insufferable Methodists in Zephyr, Ontario. They now faced the unwelcome prospect of packing up the family belongings and moving from the Leaskdale manse. Cynical about the claims made for union and embittered by the outcome of the vote, Montgomery wrote in her journal entry later that day, 'in Nature the births of living things do not take place in this fashion . . . No, 'tis no birth. It is rather the wedding of two old churches, both of whom are too old to have offspring.[8]

Sadly, too often the way the church has structured, or restructured, itself over the years has led to further disunity and bitterness between Christians rather than presenting the world with a common witness. When we study the importing of nineteenth-century Euro-stock divisions in the North American church, combined with our own domestic twentieth-century feuds,

---

8. Airhart, *The Church with the Soul of a Nation*, 3.

students instantly recognize patterns in what is happening in twenty-first-century church as we battle each other within and across denominations on issues such as worship style, language for God, and human sexuality. Teaching this history class recently I had a "1.5 generation" Korean Presbyterian student note that the Christian church in South Korea is essentially 100 years old. "Professor," he said sadly, "today we have over 100 different Presbyterian denominations in South Korea alone. Why didn't North American Presbyterians work out the problems they inherited from Scotland before exporting them to us?" Ouch. A good question. If the church is a community of sinners redeemed by grace, and saved to be sent as witnesses into the world with the healing power of the risen Christ, then what kind of model might we need going forward out of Christendom? What is the ecclesiastical framework needed today in post-Christendom when the old structures of denominationalism are breaking down?

My colleague and friend Jason Byassee names the problem specifically for the mainline churches and ecclesiology as we emerge out of Christendom.

> Mainline churches in this country [the US] were built to rule. Sometimes called the "seven sisters" (Methodist, American Baptist, Presbyterian, Lutheran, Episcopalian, Disciples of Christ, and United Church of Christ), they are heirs to the magisterial Reformation churches in Europe where they were often official state churches (Lutherans in Scandinavia; Presbyterians in Scotland and Switzerland and the Netherlands; Anglicans in England). In mid-twentieth-century America they had each built enormous infrastructure with corporate offices and heads of this and that division. They looked like a branch of the U.S. government, or a Big Three Detroit automaker, or a big box department store. . . . What do churches built to rule do with themselves when they no longer rule? When the country for which they intend to be the soul no longer knows they're there?[9]

On the one hand, denominational executives and congregational leaders with responsibilities in various judicatories naturally respond by asking questions of ecclesiology. "If we just rearrange the courts of the church or send power up to higher courts that will solve the issue." Right. The reference to church restructuring as "rearranging the deck chairs on the Titanic" has become so overused that now it's trite. On the other hand, it is easy to

---

9. Byassee, *From the Editor's Desk*, 1–2.

find those within the church who long to abandon all formal organization and simply return to the simplicity of the "early church" as our form of polity. I'm not sure people who long for a return to the early church have read carefully Paul's letters that detail such overwhelming trouble in the emerging Christian movement. No, as Darrell Guder warns, "To bemoan the emergence of the Christian movement as an organized, institutional reality is to question the essential nature of the church as a real, historical, concrete, visible witness to the Gospel. The danger of ecclesial Docetism always lurks at the edges of debates about the necessary or unnecessary nature of the church as institution."[10] At a deeper, theological level the problem is that so many church restructuring attempts begin in the wrong place. For those who love Ted Talks, you will have watched the famous "Start with Why" presentation that now has over thirty million views on YouTube, or the equivalent of the population of Canada. Not bad. Simon Sinek's Ted Talk, and book by the same name, illustrates an organizational change approach that identifies that most people begin with "what" they do, before moving onto "how" they do it as an organization but rarely get around to asking the question "why?" Sinek argues that we need to flip the script and "start with why." In Cascadia, for example, we watched the birth of the incredible global success of Starbucks. Coffee shops existed before Starbucks, of course, but Starbucks figured out what to sell and how to present it by first figuring out *why* people gather in coffee shops to begin with. They attended to why people gathered over coffee and were able to create the third space that Leonard Sweet famously promoted years ago in church circles. In his book *The Gospel According to Starbucks*, Sweet argues that Starbucks created a space that the church historically has served for community experiences between work and home. Sweet defines a third place in the following way:

> It is neutral ground.
>
> It is inclusive and promotes social equality.
>
> Conversation is the central activity.
>
> It is frequented by regulars who welcome newcomers.
>
> It is typically in a non-pretentious, homey place.
>
> It fosters a playful mood.[11]

---

10. Guder, "Taking the Form of a Servant," Laidlaw Lectures, Knox College, March 11, 2015.

11. Sweet, *The Gospel According to Starbucks*, 132.

Sinek's "start with why" approach can be helpful to us as missional disciples in post-Christendom when we explore theological categories. For example, in work that I've done resourcing judicatories over the years I've had them begin with the "why" of Christology. If we are unable to find common ground on the person and work of Christ, essentially being able to say we're on the same page about "what Jesus saves us from and what Jesus saves us for" the how and the what will go off in different directions. If the "why" is Christology, I then encourage people to reflect on the "what" of missiology. Imagine if St. Patrick landed at Saul without a clear sense of the saving work of Jesus Christ and a compelling urge to engage pre-Christians in Hibernia with this life-changing, worldview-converting, soul-freeing gospel of peace and liberation. Imagine. Surely, his ministry and the shape of the church in Ireland would have looked vastly different, if it would have even survived at all. If we begin with Christology as the why, Patrick's ministry suggests the "what" becomes missiology. In light of knowing the significance of the person and work of Jesus for our lives and the whole world, we are sent as witnesses into the world to translate the gospel into every possible culture and language. God's missiological engagement with the world through the church is what we "do" as Christians, first through the doxological lens of worshipping the Triune God and then through the missological lens of proclamation as "strangers and aliens" in this world until the kingdom comes. As a beloved saint in a former church I served once said, "Ross, I live *for* Jesus in this life until the day I get to live *with* Jesus—forever. Hallelujah." Of course, a healthy doctrine of the Trinity reminds us that we are sharing life with God right here and now by grace. As Thomas Torrance once said,

> It is distinctive of Christian theology that it treats of God in his relation to the world and of God in his relation to himself, not of one without the other. If it did not include the former, we who belong to the world could have no part in it, and if it did not include the latter, it could be concerned only with a "knowledge of God" dragged down and trapped within the world and our relations with it.[12]

The "what" of our common life in Jesus flows from worship of the Triune God out into the world as we participate with the Father, Son, and Spirit in the reconciliation of the world and the healing of the nations through our missiology. Only then can we turn to engage the question of "how"—ecclesiology

12. Torrance, *Reality and Evangelical Theology*, 21.

with a sanctified imagination. In light of who Jesus has revealed himself to be, in communion with the Father and the Spirit, "how" we are sent to be his witnesses to the ends of the earth will practically and powerfully shape what we call the church. As Darrell Guder reminds us, "missional polities are to enable the institutional church to continue the dynamic witness of the Christian movement that began at Pentecost."[13] It was only after doing this teaching with judicatories that I read Alan Hirsch's *The Forgotten Ways* for the first time and was confirmed (if not reassured!) in this approach when I discovered him saying, "we work hard to embed the following 'formula' for engaging in mission in a post-Christendom culture: *Christology determines missiology, and missiology determines ecclesiology.*"[14]

Of course, on the other hand, one of the unhelpful, knee-jerk reactions against the Christendom business model of denominationalism has been to sweep anything beyond the local congregation away. This anti-institutional approach is a popular one and, at times, creeps into missional conversations, leaving the impression that we just need to get out of (or out from underneath) the institutional church in order to practice mission. Taken to the extreme, missional theology's slogan of "joining God in the neighborhood" can even start to question the importance of the local church as long as we are out in the world living as Christians. Of course, as the social gospel offered evidence a century earlier, well-intentioned Christian movements that stray too far from the accountability of the local worshipping community and the regular doxological reframing of the culture can easily fall prey to relying on human agency alone. This is the kind of reality that gives rise to the stories preachers love to use of a pastor who visits a lapsed church member only to hear the parishioner claim that they can be a Christian without going to church. As the story goes, the pastor reaches into the roaring fire with tongs, removes a red hot coal placing it on the hearth, sits back down and watches the coal turn orange and then gray and then black and cold. The parishioner was back in church the next Sunday. All right, but it's not just about "getting people into church," it's about enlisting redeemed humanity through the worship of God out into the world to participate in God's kingdom work of reconciling the world and healing the nations. I would argue that missional theology must be careful not to

13. Guder, "Taking the Form of a Servant," Laidlaw Lectures, Knox College, March 11, 2015, 10.

14. Hirsch, *The Forgotten Ways*, 154.

succumb to the temptation of the anti-institutional approach to Christian witness. Long ago Jesuit Avery Dulles wrote,

> Christianity has always had an institutional side. It has had recognized ministers, accepted confessional formulas, and prescribed forms of public worship. All this is fitting and proper. It does not necessarily imply institutionalism, any more than papacy implies papalism, or law implies legalism, or dogma implies dogmatism. By institutionalism we mean a system in which the institutional element is treated as primary. Institutionalism is a deformation of the true nature of the Church—a deformation that has unfortunately affected the Church at certain periods of its history, and one that remains in every age a real danger to the institutional Church. A Christian believer may energetically oppose institutionalism and still be very much committed to the Church as institution.[15]

Dulles wisely cautions us away from believing that institutions in and of themselves are somehow the problem. In fact, in order to bring about meaningful change in any community or country even the most effective activist knows that institutions are required. William Wilberforce was a profound and inspired leader of the abolitionist movement that still required the "institution" of the House of Commons to end the slave trade in Britain. Nellie McClung and other faithful Christian women met in church halls across Canada and rallied for women to be recognized as persons and receive the vote, but it required the institution of the Privy Council in order to change half of humanity in this country from "non-person" to "person." Rev. Dr. Martin Luther King, Jr. led a powerful movement of the Holy Spirit at incredible cost that required the institution of the American government—including its legislative, judicial, and executive branches—in order to create lasting change.

Lesslie Newbigin famously said, "the only hermeneutic of the gospel, is a congregation of men and women who believe it and live by it."[16] Communities are formed and sustained (or not) by their hermeneutics.[17] And that provides a helpful counter-balance to the unhealthy focus on elaborate denominational structures or the dangerous "go-it-alone" tendencies found

---

15. Dulles, *Models of the Church*, 27.

16. Newbigin, *The Gospel in a Pluralist Society,* 227.

17. Branson, "Ecclesiology and Leadership for the Missional Church," in Van Gelder, ed., *The Missional Church in Context*, 95.

in some Christian circles that see the church as an obstacle for change in the world. Indian Missiologist Paul Joshua Bhakiaraj argues:

> The church catholic exists first and foremost at the level of a local community. Denominational structures and church hierarchies might be helpful, but a missionary ecclesiology is found practiced in a local church. Constituted by the Father, Son and Holy Spirit, the church living its life in the Trinity and according to that pattern, cannot be something other than a social, self-giving loving community in union with God and in fellowship with one another.[18]

Andy Root notes the shift in modernity from our reliance on local communities to what he calls "zombie institutions." Root notes that for most of human history "widows and orphans were to be cared for by uncles, aunts, and neighbors. Their emotional, but most fundamentally their basic financial and material needs were the responsibility of those who knew them and were part of their story."[19] Of course, another outcome of modernity is the greater mobility of people today that takes them farther and farther from their communities of origin. Root is clear, we need institutions to take care of us but how might we take steps to recover the crucial role of communities of accountability and compassion?

Therefore, the church simply as an institution is not a bad thing. The question becomes, what kind of institution shall it be in accordance with the witness of Scripture and the guidance of the Holy Spirit? Dulles defined institutionalism as a deformity of the true church where the church itself becomes the focus. Darrell Guder picks up on this theme when he writes,

> The church is not the ultimate and intended outcome of God's grace. Christ did not die only to save Christians, nor to form a church of the saved, but to bring God's healing love to the world. The formation of the church and the salvation of its members are the "first fruits" of God's desire for all creation. Mission, therefore, must not be reduced to institutional preservation, or in terms of today's crisis of church in the West, its survival. It's faithful witness takes place as the church submits to Christ's lordship and carries out his work wherever he sends it. The church does not point to itself, but to Christ, following the model of John the Baptist, "He must increase, so I must decrease."[20]

18. Bhakiaraj, "Mission of the Local Church?," in Haokip and Imchen, eds., *Becoming a Missional Congregation in the Twenty-First Indian Context*, 48.

19. Root, *The Promise of Despair*, 47.

20. Guder, *Incarnation and the Church's Witness*, 23–24.

Like being cast as an innkeeper instead of Mary in a church Christmas pageant, it can be hard, given our human sinfulness, to move aside and accept our role as the one who points to Jesus in a John-the-Baptist-like role. But imagine a church where instead of someone shaking hands at the door saying, "What a great sermon, pastor" they say instead, "What a great God!" Guder's challenge to us that mission cannot be reduced to institutional preservation is especially apt for the mainline church that since the 1960s has been retooling its structures in order to accommodate for decline. On a congregational level it looks something like a church I served where the minister's wife started an annual flea market in the 1960s. At the time, 100 percent of the proceeds from the rummage sale or flea market were given away for missions at home and abroad. By the time I arrived as pastor decades later, the flea market was running twice a year and 100 percent of the proceeds were kept for the congregation to pay its bills, "including your salary, Reverend" as church members would often remind me when I questioned the objective, outcome, and output of what had essentially become a congregational idol. What began in mission to the world had now become a millstone around the neck of this congregation. The two flea markets produced nearly $100,000 a year in revenue for the church. "How could we possibly live without it now, pastor?" people asked. More than the money issue, however, was the fact that members of the church were spending many days a week, year-round, in the dark church basement that had been taken over by this internal fundraiser so that the space could not be used for Christian programming and these Christians were spending their time sorting clothes and antiques rather than being equipped and sent as missionary disciples into the world! Missional polity pushes back against a church that exists for itself, as Guder warns, "Where the church is an end in itself, its polity becomes a divine institution that exists for its own sake."[21]

Andrew Purves reminds us, "The ministry of the church is our participation in the continuing ministry of Jesus Christ, to the glory of the Father, in the power of the Holy Spirit."[22] I'm not sure Jesus spent a lot of time on fundraisers for the local synagogue. No, our ministries and mission as a church are intimately tied up in the ongoing redemptive work of the Triune God in the world. Often our structures from the local level through various judicatories to national courts of the church are now like that flea

21. Guder, "Taking the Form of a Servant," Laidlaw Lectures, Knox College, March 11, 2015, 12.

22. Purves, *Reconstructing Pastoral Theology*, 10.

market, working furiously at maintaining the institution rather than joining God in the mission of reconciliation in the world. My colleague Ross Hastings names the missiological problem in North America as moving from inculturation to enculturation. Inculturation is a missiological term "which refers to ways to adapt the communication of the gospel for a specific culture being evangelized."[23] Enculturation, on the other hand, is a process of influence by the dominant culture upon "an individual or community (e.g., the church) to imbibe its accepted norms and values so the individual or community is pressured to find acceptance within the society of that culture."[24] Hastings balances the positive aspects of culture (creation of humankind in the image of God) with the demonic corruption of culture (the fall of humankind) on the other. He names the tension by stating, "The challenge the Western church faces is that it is often encultured in ways that it ought not to be, and that it is not inculturating the gospel in ways it ought to be."[25] A local congregation today that spends most of its energy simply making money to keep the doors open, the organ playing, and paid soloist singing in Latin is living with a different sense of call than the gospel demands. As Darrell Guder reminds us, "The incarnational character of the church is rooted, not in its alleged perfection, but in its submission to Jesus Christ. Its identity is defined by its relationship to Jesus Christ. That is why the followers of Jesus came to be called, 'Christians' (Acts 11:26), that is 'Christ's persons.'"[26] A church built on the understanding of every person being "Christ's persons" will have a much clearer sense of mission and purpose then we find within the structures of the mainline church in North America today. My colleague Jonathan Wilson describes what a healthy evangelical ecclesiology might look like when he writes:

> Called into being by the good news of Jesus Christ and empowered for witness to that gospel, the evangelical church needs to maintain a missional ecclesiology, with its commitment to mission and concomitant flexibility, while also remaining faithful to our commission. The best way to describe this and equip ourselves for faithful flexibility is to add to our missional ecclesiology an improvisational ecclesiology. When evangelical ecclesiology is improvisational, it enables the church to fulfill its mission in changing

---

23. Hastings, *Missional God, Missional Church*, 38.

24. Ibid.

25. Ibid.

26. Guder, *Incarnation and the Church's Witness*, 23.

circumstances. . . . An improvisational ecclesiology recognizes the demands of adaptation and faithfulness and commits us to both. We must learn properly to confess in word and deed that the church is one, holy, catholic and apostolic.[27]

So what does this clarity of mission affecting the structure of an organization look like? I recently discovered an example in a most unlikely place.

After several years without a furry friend, our family made the fateful decision one summer to adopt a cat. Previously a dog-friendly family, our strata bylaws in North Vancouver made it clear that only a cat would do. We began our search online and saw the various dodgy websites advertising pets for sale. Then we stumbled upon an organization called VOKRA. "What's that?" I asked myself, thinking it sounded vaguely like a super villain organization from the James Bond franchise. "The Vancouver Orphaned Kitten Rescue Association," my wife replied. "That's quite a handle," I conceded and agreed to check it out. What followed next taught this eager missiologist a few lessons about what the church should look like in society.

First, I visited their excellent and informative website and filled out an application for adoption. Next, I was contacted immediately by a volunteer asking for a good time to chat on the phone to explain the mission of the organization. I soon found myself talking with the most delightful woman who clearly articulated the vision, mission, and goals of the organization without hesitation. She even added a little testimony about how her life was changed by adopting cats through VOKRA and she decided to give of her time to volunteer so that others could experience "the good news." She explained how there are 400 foster homes for orphaned cats in our city and soon set us up for a house visit with a potential new cat friend for our family.

A couple of days later we found ourselves in the home of two lovely young women who foster cats on behalf of VOKRA. Again, they could easily and convincingly describe both the purpose of the organization and why their involvement was so important on a personal level. The cat was perfect for our active family and so we found ourselves the following day meeting with yet *another* volunteer (proudly wearing her VOKRA t-shirt) at a neighborhood Starbucks, where we went through a home assessment, transition plan, and paperwork to pay and adopt this stray cat. You've already guessed. The normal, lovely volunteer took time to talk about why the organization

27. Wilson, *Why Church Matters*, 153.

matters to the life of our city and then added some personal narrative about her experiences of rescuing cats and matching them with loving homes.

So, we now have Rosie the cat, who is playful, charming and a wonderful addition to our home. But in addition to that, I was left in awe of this rescue organization in our city. Completely staffed by volunteers who understood their work to be urgent, transformative, and life-giving (salvific?) not just for the individual (cat/owner) but also for the welfare of the whole city. Hmm. Here I am an ordained pastor in the Reformed tradition and I'm not sure many of our churchgoers could give such a clear and passionate description of the rescue mission God has given ambassadors of Christ through the gospel. Imagine, if the church could know itself in such clear missional terms and in response to the Holy Spirit's prompting declare the gospel to be so urgently needed for the salvation and welfare of the community. Clearly it's time for some missiological lessons from our cat friends—of which, now I am one.

Clarity on mission will impact an organization's structure and purpose. There are hopeful signs as denominations pay closer attention to the connection between missiology and ecclesiology. One example is the discernment and decision-making within the Dutch Reformed Church (DRC) in South Africa, which has been taking steps over several years towards becoming a missional church in structure and practice. At the congregational level, local churches are exploring "missional ecclesiology" and experimenting with what it means to be the sent people of God in the world. At the regional synod level resources have been freed up for church planting and supporting new expressions of church while paying better attention to the struggle between gospel and culture. At the general synod level the church agreed to "apply itself with renewed vigor, courage and determination—in light of God's work in the world (Missio Dei), and the church's missional calling and responsibility (Missio ecclesiae)."[28] Within the document the DRC attempts to name the implications for the church as the missional community of God.

> This placement of the church within the missio Dei has fundamental consequences: The church is mission and participates in God's mission. It simply cannot be anything other than that! That is precisely the reason for the church's existence—the church was created with this exactly (and only) this purpose in mind. The

28. The Framework Document on the Missional Nature and Calling of the Dutch Reformed Church, 2.

mission as it comes forth from God's mouth is the mission of the church. The church is the result, the fruition, of God's mission, and therefore exists to take part in this mission and be of service to ensure its continuation. This is the heart and the being of the church, and that is why it is SO essential that the mission of the church not stop with its completion—reaching out to and serving others will be part and parcel of everlasting life. Mission is the way the church lives. The church is called to be a "sign" of God's Kingdom, giving those around them a little taste of God's healing sovereignty. As church, as sent/missional congregations, we are gathered, formed and sent out to carry the message of God's love further into the world.[29]

The DRC is out in front of other denominations in naming the reality of the shift from Christendom to post-Christendom and actively pursuing questions of what this means for the mission and ministry of the church. The DRC's study and reflection on becoming a missional church includes a series of "New Insights" on their understanding of God, the church, the kingdom of God, incarnation, the world, congregations, being servants in the community, faith formation, offices of the church, church planting, liturgy, youth ministry and catechesis, public witness, theological education, and church order. This comprehensive approach to missional ecclesiology is encouraging as a traditional denomination seeks to travel lightly as workers in God's harvest, speaking peace like the disciples of old in Luke 10. The DRC offers an example of an ecclesiastical body reshaping itself as a humble witness pointing towards Jesus. As Darrell Guder contends, "What the world should experience in the church is not perfect Christians, but honest Christians whose lives enflesh the real possibility of new life, a new creation, living hope, and confidence that "the one who began a good work among you will bring it to complete by the day of Jesus Christ."[30] No longer will mission be subsumed under ecclesiology as one of many "departments" of the church. No, the missional church "shifts the focus to the world as the horizon for understanding the work of God and the identity of the church . . . .The relationship of the *mission Dei* (the larger mission of God) to the *kingdom of God* (the redemptive reign of God in Christ)."[31]

29. The Framework Document on the Missional Nature and Calling of the Dutch Reformed Church, 5.

30. Guder, *Incarnation and the Church's Witness*, 23, citing Philippians 1:6.

31. Van Gelder, *The Ministry of the Missional Church*, 86.

This turning not only shifts the church's focus to the world but it sets that "horizon of understanding" within the narrative arc of God's redemptive plan. As the church moves out of Christendom and away from courting earthly power, living as a missional community for the sake of the world, our ecclesiology is profoundly shaped by an eschatological vision. The jury is *not* out. In fact, the verdict is in. We know how this will all end. We cling to the promise of God's fulfillment of redemption he began at Creation, revealed in covenant with Israel, made clear in the cross, proclaims through the church down the ages, and will bring to fulfillment in consummation with Christ's return. We read in Philippians, "being confident in this, that he who began a good work in you carry it on to completion in Christ Jesus."[32] Do we realize in our current denominational silos that one day the name "Presbyterian, Catholic, Baptist or Anglican" will mean nothing, as the only name upon our lips will be Jesus as we confess him as Lord of all to the glory of God the Father?[33] How might that truth, that promise, that future-orientated gift shape the way we organize, fund, live, and lead as a community of missionary disciples today?

32. Phil 1:6, *NIV.*
33. Phil 2:11, *NIV.*

CHAPTER NINE

Monasterboice

New Monasticism

*The restoration of the church will surely come only from
a new type of monasticism which has nothing in common
with the old but a complete lack of compromise in a life
lived in accordance with the Sermon on the Mount in the
discipleship of Christ. I think it is time to gather people
together to do this.*

—DIETRICH BONHOEFFER

AFTER RAY AND LUKE Skywalker met face to face on Skellig Michael in
the final scene of *Star Wars: The Force Awakens*, the whole world caught a
glimpse of the stunning beauty and rugged remoteness of Irish monastic
sites. There was something oddly appropriate for a Hollywood quasi-reli-
gious figure such as a Jedi Knight to be depicted in an isolated retreat from
the universe on a traditional site of Irish monasticism. Indeed, a thirteenth-
century German source claimed that Skellig was the final location of the
battle between St. Patrick and the venomous snakes and devils that plagued
Ireland. Well, maybe not, but there is no doubt that Patrick's ministry
helped establish the essential foundations for the future flourishing of the
monastic movement in Ireland.

One of those sites that *Star Wars* fans have not yet discovered is
Monasterboice. Tucked off the M1 motorway between Belfast and Dublin just north of Drogheda, the historic ruins of Monasterboice tell of a
story of an early Christian settlement founded in the late fifth century by

Saint Buithe, who died around 521 AD. Buithe, an apprentice of Patrick, represents the second generation of leaders for the Irish church, who established monastic settlements across the Island. Today, you can still see the old round tower and spectacular high crosses (the highest in Ireland) that tell of great biblical stories carved into their stone bodies, almost as our Cascadian West Coast Salish Indigenous peoples carve stories into tall trees known as totem poles.

Very little is known about Monasterboice's founder, Saint Buithe. A single text of the saint survives, but is an edited edition of two earlier sources. It tells of his life, beginning with various miracles throughout his childhood and ending close to the point of his death with his prophecy concerning the birth of Colum Cille, who was later said to visit the site. Buithe was a devoted follower of Saint Patrick and settled in this area to help with the bishop's missionary work—presumably quite late in his life. His birth was supposed to have been proceeded by fire in the sky as a good omen of God's work. And the saint's "manner and habit of life" was said to bear a close resemblance to the charism of Saint Brigid. He was a descendant of one of the chieftains of Munster. He is said to have travelled extensively throughout Germany, Italy, and England before finally settling in Ireland. Two stories tell of miracles in his life and influence. In an echo of Jesus' healing the blind man in John 9 and sending him to the pool of Siloam, Buithe encounters a blind man who asks for healing. St. Buithe tells him to wash his eyes in a nearby holy well. The man does so and is miraculously healed. The other tale, this one an echo of Moses' liberation of the Hebrew slaves from Egypt, tells of how an important visitor needed to get across the River Boyne, which was swollen in flood and highly dangerous. So Buithe struck the waters and they parted like the Red Sea, allowing safe passage for the important visitor. The historicity of these hagiographic stories matters less than the fascinating witness of these new monastic communities in a pagan land.

Patrick's founding of monasteries and convents in Ireland, alongside the development of the more traditional parish model with ordained priests, was very much in line with the growth of the monastic movement in the rest of the church throughout the Roman Empire. Onward from Emperor Constantine's embrace of Christianity in the fourth century, small groups of celibate Christian men and women had gathered in communities to pursue their spiritual goals.

The pioneers in this movement were Anthony and Pachomius in Egypt, who organized the first monasteries in the desert based on work and worship governed by a common rule. This sort of group ascetic life soon spread throughout the Near East, then west to Italy, Spain and Gaul. From the beginning, communities of women were an important part of the monastic movement.[1]

Celtic Monasteries became known over time as places of prayer and launching pads for evangelistic missions. Perhaps the best known of these is the voyage of Brendan, which tells the tale of sixth-century Irish monks on an adventure that brings them into contact with holy men, sea monsters, and talking birds. Lacking the desert wastelands to which their Christian brothers and sisters of Egypt and the Middle East withdrew, many Irish monks instead went on voyages as an act of spiritual discipline.[2] Irish monks became associated with the phrase, "the cell and the coracle," whereby the cell was the place of contemplative prayer alone with God and in community worship, while the coracle referred to a round, flat-bottomed boat made from woven wood covered in skins that bore them on evangelistic missions to distant lands.[3] The rapid growth of monastic settlements in the century following Patrick's death, and the accompanying establishment of thriving "scriptoria," is incredible given the world that Patrick first evangelized. Alannah Hopkin notes, "It is remarkable, given the non-literate state of pagan Irish society, that by around 500 AD distinctively Hiberno-Latin writings of high quality were being produced."[4]

To walk in the ruins of Monasterboice today is to wonder about what life together means for us in a post-Christendom Cascadia. It is curious how the new monastic movement has taken root here in Cascadia. I am always fascinated by visits to intentional Christian communities throughout the Pacific Northwest, and I am in awe of these Christians who are living humble, simple, meaningful lives that turn away from the highly consumeristic and individualistic values of the dominant culture.

If Christendom established and encouraged a certain "witness protection program" for too many church members in the history of the West, new monasticism is unmasking the presence of Christians in the midst of ordinary neighborhoods. With a debt of gratitude to pioneers like Shane

1. Freeman, *The World of Saint Patrick*, 5.

2. Ibid., 129.

3. Frost and Hirsch, *The Faith of Leap*, 103–4.

4. Hopkin, *The Living Legend of Patrick*, 54.

Claiborne and Jonathan Wilson-Hartgrove, many Christians have re-ordered and reconstituted their common life together along the lines of the twelve marks of new nonasticism.[5] At St. Andrew's Hall where I teach, we've begun a new monastic experiment of our own. Taking two of our townhouse residences and remaking them into the "Salt and Light experiment" along the lines of Matthew 5, we're exploring what it means to have Christians living intentionally together in order to be salt and light on the university campus. We're trying to live into what Jesus meant by his inspiring but challenging message in the Sermon on the Mount:

> You are the salt of the earth. But if the salt loses its saltiness, how can it be made salty again? It is no longer good for anything, except to be thrown out and trampled underfoot. You are the light of the world. A town built on a hill cannot be hidden. Neither do people light a lamp and put it under a bowl. Instead they put it on its stand, and it gives light to everyone in the house. In the same way, let your light shine before others, that they may see your good deeds and glorify your Father in heaven.[6]

In this experiment, three men (Light house) and three women (Salt house) live according to a rule of faith based on *prayer, hospitality, and witness* as well as a rule of life to govern their common space. In a sense, it feels like petri dish ecclesiology, observing how Christians form community and share life together in the name of Jesus Christ.

It is one small step in Cascadia to end the "witness protection program" of Christendom and invite conversation and engagement with neighbors in the heart of our college community. I was reminded of the need for Christians in a minority status within the post-Christian Pacific Northwest culture during a year when we received an unusually cold blast of winter.

If you've ever spent a winter in Vancouver or Seattle you'll know that there is very little salt *or* light. Having grown up in the frigid yet beautiful prairie landscape of Winnipeg, I know that most Canadians experience a

---

5. These marks include relocation to the abandoned places of empire, sharing economic resources with fellow members, humble submission to the church, geographical proximity to community members who share a common rule of life, hospitality to the stranger, nurturing common life among members of intentional community, peacemaking in the midst of violence, lament for racial divisions, care for the earth, support for celibate singles alongside monogamous married couples and their children, intentional formation in the way of Christ and the rule of the community, and commitment to a disciplined contemplative life.

6. Matt 5:13–16, *NIV.*

great dose of both salt and light. Salt, liberally spread on the icy roads in the winter to keep driving and walking safe. Light, on the other hand, in the brilliant reflection of the winter sun on snow-covered fields and roofs, which lifts people's spirits and has them say things like, "Well, it's a dry cold."

Most winters in Vancouver have neither salt nor light. There is no need for salt on the roads where it only dips below freezing every few years. There is no light in the winter as dark and stormy rain clouds hover over the Pacific Northwest from Portland to Port Moody, mid-autumn to early spring. But every now and then there is a surprise.

I remember flying out of Vancouver in December 2008 just before the last big snowstorm shut down the city. Sure, we've had a bit of snow since then over the years. It comes for a day or two and then melts. Frosty the snowman has a short shelf life here on the West Coast. This one year in particular that I'm thinking about, however, was different. Snow started falling (and stayed on the ground!) on December fifth. Over three months later there were still beautiful large, white snowflakes dancing down from the sky. The snow was bright and beautiful coloring over green golf courses, crushing startled palm trees and blanketing distant mountain peaks. Yes, for a change there was light in Vancouver that winter. But it also became obvious that there was not as much salt as some people believed they needed.

Within a short period of time the region was running low on salt and residents began griping that back streets were not ploughed properly and alleyways and sidewalks were being turned into skating rinks. The City of Vancouver responded by offering free salt in large piles in front of local fire halls. And what was the newsworthy result? Humanity's flaws were on display for the whole nation to see.

While listening to Vancouverites complain about icy streets and -1 degree Celsius weather was embarrassing to me and hilarious to the rest of the country, sights and sounds from local media outlets watching people fighting over limited free salt were not so entertaining. For some, it seemed inconceivable that in polite, refined urban Canada, citizens could be shoving and yelling at others, jumping queues or letting their tempers flair to the point where police have to intervene. I suppose the two Stanley Cup riots in Vancouver when our Canucks hockey team lost were not seen as a warning sign for those handing out salt in the streets. And yet, as a Reformed Christian, one of my favorite doctrines has long been total human depravity. Yes, when Jesus got a hold of me as a teenager part of my submission to him was taking stock of the competing truth claims swirling around me. On the one hand, the world claimed a story that "deep down we're good people and can solve our own problems." The gospel, however, presented a very different story to live by. The gospel claims that deep down we're messed up and selfish, sinful and broken, and need a Savior to rescue us. Well, it was pretty clear around me *and inside me* that the truth claims of the gospel were truer than the naïve optimism of human progress that the world and its self-help gurus wanted me to buy into. Total human depravity as a reality and the gospel as a remedy—our need for a loving, redeeming Savior to save us from ourselves—that's a story worth giving one's life to. And there it was, on full display that winter, as neighbor fought neighbor for free salt. I don't think I was the only one who wondered what might happen when the long anticipated big earthquake eventually strikes this region. If we can't even share salt with our neighbor, what will happen when buildings collapse, bridges fail, and our food and water supplies run low? Lord, have mercy.

Times like that are a great opportunity for followers of Jesus to ask themselves how their devotion to Christ might translate into something visible—salt and light for those around them. Tina Block notes from her interviews with Pacific Northwest secular residents that many were turned off the Christian faith due to the hypocrisy they witnessed from church people. Block finds, in an interview with a woman who grew up in a small Washington State town, a familiar objection to Christianity: "living in that small town and seeing the hypocrites that were lined up at the church door on Sunday, and were out with somebody else's wife on Saturday night, or were mistreating their employees . . ." was enough to turn someone off to Christian community.[7] New monastic communities serve to break down the stereotypes sadly earned by the church over the post-war years when "cultural Christianity" was the dominant and visible form of ecclesiology. Cultural Christianity is rapidly dying (and most profoundly affecting the mainline liberal Protestant churches) and it simply cannot die fast enough. The Triune God calls people today not to a cultural Christianity that equates good citizenship with good Christianity, but rather to a passionate following of Jesus in our everyday, ordinary lives. This movement uses our simple words and actions as a witness to Christ's love in this broken yet beautiful world. Jonathan Wilson notes that new monasticism is not a retreat from the world but rather a reforming of Christian witness in light of Christendom baggage.

7. Block, *Secular Northwest*, 62.

The very mission of the church calls us to be in the world as witnesses of the redemptive power of the Gospel. Nevertheless, there are times—and I have argued that this is one of them—when the life of the church as been so compromised that we no longer are capable of fulfilling faithfully our mission. At such a time, the church must withdraw into a new monasticism, not in order to avoid a bad society, but in order to recover faithful living and a renewed understanding of the church's mission.[8]

We are being called once more as a minority to reflect Jesus' salt and light in the world. Many are discovering that this is an opportune time to speak and act as those living with full awareness of the covenant of grace and sharing an abiding love in the one who is the Mediator of that same covenant. This is a great season to be seasoned by the Savior and shine the light of Christ in our communities, trusting that the darkness cannot overcome it.

I visited recently with the Emmaus Community in Victoria, led by former students of mine at the Vancouver School of Theology. Operating out of a beautiful old early twentieth-century home in the Fernwood neighborhood of the city, the Emmaus Community has been building relationships and practicing attentiveness to God's faithful presence in a city that is highly secular and neo-pagan. The Emmaus Community is based on a Rule of Life they describe in this way:

> The Emmaus Community is a New Monastic community
>
> whose recognition of Christ in our midst
>
> leads us to walk the Way of love
>
> through prayer, simplicity and
>
> presence with each other and in our neighbourhood.

They have established two different forms of belonging to the community. The broader of the two categories is designed for those who live at a geographic distance from the home and who are unable to commit to the more rigorous demands of community life. They are known as companions of the Emmaus Community. Companion members have discerned a call to Christian community and in particular to the ethos, rule, and founding Scripture of the Emmaus Community. They are invited to unite their lives of prayer, simplicity, and presence to that of the Emmaus Community but are called to live this out in the context of their own particular

8. Wilson, *Living Faithfully in a Fragmented World*, 59.

neighborhoods, congregations, and vocations. While geographically apart from the new monastic community, they still undergo a period of discernment and formation in dialogue with the formation director in order to establish a modified personal rule/rhythm of life modeled on that of the Emmaus Community and rooted in their baptismal covenant. Companion members attend community events as they are able and support the community through prayer and other forms of giving, including financial offering.

For those who live within walking distance of the Belmont Avenue house, and feel called to a more regular commitment to life together, there is the invitation to apply to be a covenanted member. Covenanted members are baptized individuals over sixteen years old who feel called to the specific form of Christian community embodied in the founding Scripture and rhythm and rule of life of the Emmaus Community. They are ready to unite their lives of prayer, simplicity, and presence with the community and feel called to live/be a tangible presence within or near the geographic location of the Emmaus Community. Covenanted members enter into a formal period of formation/discernment for nine months to one year (novice period) and, in consultation with the community, discern if they are called to a life of Christian discipleship in the Emmaus Community. In addition, admission to the covenanted member status must come with a letter from a spiritual mentor such as a pastor affirming this vocation, as well as a letter of support from a spouse/partner who is not entering the community (if applicable). In making their vows of prayer, simplicity, and presence covenanted members are held accountable to the community in engaging the rhythm and rule of life. The first vows taken are for a year and then a commitment is renewed for five years. Covenanted members participate in the decision-making and organizational structure of the community while sharing in the responsibility for mentoring and nurturing new community members.[9]

The weekend I visited with my friends in the Emmaus Community I followed their rhythm of life, from morning prayer to hosting a coffee party for a mix of neighborhood folks ranging from the homeless to young mothers, to an afternoon spent helping with their monastic brewing complete with hand pumped water from a local well. The worship throughout the day, combined with service and community meals, helped reveal the appeal of these new monastic communities where, like the monastic

9. www.emmauscommunity.ca.

communities of old in Hibernia, these Cascadian cousins operate on their own time and biblically distinct values. New monasticism is not an escape from the world, but rather a different way of living *in* the world and engaging God and neighbor for the sake of that same evangelistic witness and missionary discipleship that we find in church planting as well. Jonathan Wilson suggests that these new monastic communities are marked by a "recovery of the telos"—understanding their whole lives as being lived under the Lordship of Christ, that it is for the whole people of God and not just religious elites, and that it will be marked by a commitment to discipline and Christian practice, as well as undergirded by deep theological reflection and commitment.[10]

Leaders in these new monastic communities are weary of claims that this kind of intense Christian community is the only way of the future in a post-Christendom world. It is a special calling and not for everyone, but just as the monasteries of Hibernia supported the wider church and community as places of study, prayer and service, so too new monastic communities in Cascadia provide a gift to the wider body of believers who are seeking to be a faithful witness in their every day lives, at home, work, and school.

10. Wilson, *Living Faithfully in a Fragmented World*, 60–62.

CHAPTER TEN

Ail

Social Justice

Life as we know it, with all its ups and downs, will soon be over.
We all will give an accounting to God of how we have lived.
You may choose to look the other way
but you can never say again that you did not know.

—WILLIAM WILBERFORCE

WHILE PATRICK'S BETTER KNOWN writing entitled *Confession* was most likely written near the end of his life, trying to swipe away detractors and cement his ministry's place within the larger church, the "Letter to the Soldiers of Coroticus" is from a younger Patrick responding to an immediate pastoral crisis that provoked a deep sense of injustice. In this short dispatch, Patrick is furious that soldiers loyal to Coroticus, a Roman Britain warlord who was nominally Christian, attacked a number of Patrick's newly baptized converts and carried them off into slavery while they were still wearing their white baptismal gowns with chrism oil shining on their foreheads. The Irish bishop's passion in the letter no doubt comes out of his deep empathy for these newly baptized noviates, as they are "Patrick in reverse"—having been taking as slaves from Ireland to Britain. And this time instead of pagan pirates seizing Christians it's "Christian" pirates seizing fellow Christians.

In the vacuum of power left by the retreating Roman legions, warlords emerged and grabbed whatever there was for the taking, including people, who were kidnapped and then held for ransom or sold into slavery.

Coroticus was one of those warlords.[11] Ironically, many of the warlords like Coroticus were of Patrick's old social station in Britain, former Roman nobles who went from town councilors to tyrants. Patrick addresses the warlord using his Latin name, and while precisely identifying whether Coroticus was Welsh or Scottish has been a matter of debate amongst scholars, there is some evidence that would lead us to the latter rather than the former. The suggestion that Coroticus was from the Strathclyde region of what we now called Scotland today comes from Muirchu's *Life of Patrick*, written in the seventh century and on display today in *The Book of Armagh* in Trinity College, Dublin, alongside its more famous cousin *The Book of Kells*. In Muirchu's *Life of Patrick* it reads, "Of holy Patrick's stand against Coirthech, king of Ail." It is believe that the king or chieftain of Ail (from which this chapter takes its name) was the destination of Patrick's newly baptized slaves, somewhere around Dumbarton on the Clyde. It's believed, therefore, that Coirthech/Coroticus in Patrick's letter ruled close to the Picts.[12] Theories abound, of course, as to the real identity of Coroticus, with one scholar even suggesting he may have been a Roman Briton living in Ireland.[13] While it is still a matter of debate amongst scholars whether this Coirthech of Ail is the source of Patrick's holy anger, it makes the most sense to a number of scholars that the slave-king would be located close to the Picts, in light of Patrick's letter that lumps Coroticus and his soldiers in with that tribe. Patrick writes

> I cannot say that they are my fellow-citizens, nor fellow-citizens of the saints of Rome, but fellow-citizens of demons, because of their evil works. By their hostile ways they live in death, allies of the apostate Scots and Picts. They are blood-stained: blood-stained with the blood of innocent Christians, whose numbers I have given birth to in God and confirmed in Christ.[14]

Patrick's *Letter to Coroticus* is a stinging, direct, and passionate plea where the Irish saint writes to a powerful leader in his former homeland warning

---

11. Coroticus (Latinized form of the British name Ceretic) appears in fifth-century records and was ascribed to two different warlords, one based in Wales, the other in Scotland.

12. The term *Pict* or *Picti* meant "painted one" and was the name given by the Romans to the tribes in Scotland living north of the Clyde River.

13. Thompson, *Who was Saint Patrick?*, 136.

14. Patrick, *Letter to the Soldiers of Coroticus*, Section 2; in Patrick, *Confessio and Epistola*.

that their actions serve as a rejection of their own baptismal vows, God's grace-filled gift of life rejected in blood and an open rebellion against the Triune God.

Patrick records his reaction to news of the attack on his newly baptized Irish Christians in this way:

> The very next day after my new converts, dressed all in white, were anointed with chrism, even as it was still gleaming upon their foreheads, they were cruelly cut down and killed by the swords of these same devilish men. At once I sent a good priest with a letter. I could trust him, for I had taught him from his boyhood. He went, accompanied by other priests, to see if we might claw something back from all the looting, most important, the baptized captives whom they had seized. Yet all they did was to laugh in our faces at the mere mention of their prisoners.[15]

Patrick was enraged with holy fury, seething at the injustice of his newly baptized Christians suffering abuse and captivity at the hands of so called "Christian Roman Britons." Patrick knew first-hand how brutal slave traders were and how they operated. Says Thomas O'Loughlin, "slavers preferred to capture women who could serve their masters in field, household and bed; next, they preferred boys who could work hard and not be too truculent; and lastly, adult males caught on a slaving expedition would probably be put to the sword."[16] Patrick writes this letter picturing his recently baptized men pierced by the sword and drawing their last breath, women dragged off to suffer unspeakable horrors, and young boys condemned to a life of hard service. In response, Patrick launches his own attack upon the soldiers using words that are meant to sting and declare them unfit for civilized society.

> Because of all this, I am at a loss to know whether to weep more for those they killed or those that are captured: or indeed for these men themselves whom the devil has taken fast for his slaves. In truth, they will bind themselves alongside him in the pains of the everlasting pit: for "he who sins is a slave already" and is to be called "son of the devil." Because of this, let every God-fearing man mark well that to me they are outcasts: cast out also by Christ my God, whose ambassador I am.[17]

15. Patrick, *Letter to the Soldiers of Coroticus*, Section 3, in Patrick, *Confessio and Epistola*.

16. O'Loughlin, *Discovering Saint Patrick*, 36.

17. Patrick, *Letter to the Soldiers of Coroticus*, Section 4, in Patrick, *Confessio and*

Patrick essentially writes the letter for any church leader in Britain who would read it as an excommunication of Coroticus from the church. The outcome of Patrick's letter is unknown. It is unlikely any church authority had the moral courage to take action against Coroticus back in Britain as the social fabric of the society was breaking down and the church needed its own protectors. In fact, it has been suggested that Patrick's actions against Coroticus may have put him in some hot water. As D. R. Howlett states, "Patrick's attempt as a bishop *Hiberione constitutus* to excommunicate from Ireland a tyrant in Britain may have provoked British ecclesiastical authorities to try and condemn him in his absence."[18] In many ways, Patrick was out of step with his clerical colleagues in the wider church when it came to his Christian care for those unlike himself. While Patrick felt a divine call to carry the gospel to those outside the Roman Empire, he was in the minority by doing so. As Daniel Conneely argues,

> Missions to barbarians outside the Roman frontiers were not a feature of the early Church. From his Letter excommunicating Coroticus we know that many Britons looked askance at the mission to the Irish, indeed some were hostile to the very idea of it. We can understand, if we cannot respect the grounds for this. Britain had been Romanized (which in that age mean, for the western world, civilized) for some centuries. Ireland, never Romanized, was a barbarian island. Its people, barbarians, were regarded as, thereby, inferior.[19]

Patrick's passionate communication in the *Letter to Coroticus* reminds us of the need for missional leaders to speak up and speak out against injustice in our context as well. This call of the gospel to speak against injustice can so easily be dismissed, however, from a post-Christendom culture that has stopped listening to the moral authority of the church.

"It's a good thing." Martha Stewart is famous for this phrase, but apparently it doesn't apply to preaching. At least according to a curious interview in *The Globe and Mail* where, reflecting on her brand's global impact, she stated:

> I was raised by two schoolteachers so we were always being taught. We were taught to respect education and our teachers. And I loved my teachers. I remember all their names and used to have them

---

Epistola.

18. Howlett, *The Book of Letters of Saint Patrick the Bishop*, 119.

19. Conneely, *St. Patrick's Letters*, 120.

over for lunch at my house. Teaching is very important. But I'm not a preacher. I want to make that very clear: We don't preach. We teach.[20]

As a preacher, I always find it interesting how quickly people associate preaching with a pejorative meaning. I also find it curious how people assume that teaching and preaching are set in opposition to one another. Curious, since in the Reformed tradition we call our ordained ministers "teaching elders." As a teaching elder in the Presbyterian Church in Canada, for example, I understand my role as a preacher in terms of Ephesians 4: 12, "to equip the saints for the work of ministry, for building up the body of Christ." This equipping is teaching, it is training God's people to be witnesses to the resurrection in the world. Preaching the Word of God declares that sinful, broken human beings are saved by the grace of Jesus Christ for a purpose—we are saved to serve. As a professor, pastor and preacher, I take seriously the role given to me as a "teaching elder."

I have a hunch that the pejorative association with the word *preaching* has to do with stereotypes of wild-eyed preachers in cheap suits hurling "hellfire and brimstone" from the pulpit. I get it. And yet, there is always a cutting edge to the Word of God preached, a reality of spiritual warfare and the need for a prophetic voice. In a post-Christendom North America preaching may no longer have the privileged place it once held in broader society. In our evangelical, Reformed witness, however, we continue to preach and teach the Word of God while participating in the redeeming and reconciling ministry of Christ in this world. As Abraham Kuyper so famously said, "There is not a square inch in the whole domain of our human existence over which Christ, who is Sovereign over all, does not cry, Mine!" Today, in post-Christendom, we hear that as a minority more as a promise of an eschatological vision rather than a project with political power that we might accomplish through human agency. So yes, "It's a good thing."

One of the roles of preaching in a post-Christendom context, like a pre-Christian one, is the urgent need for a prophetic witness. Not only are we called to proclaim Jesus Christ, crucified and risen, but we are commissioned by God to be clear on *who* this resurrected Christ is—not a Savior of our own making.

I recall leading a pilgrimage tour years ago in Jordan. We found ourselves at Mt. Nebo and had the opportunity to read the story of the death of Moses and Joshua leading the people into the promised land. We stopped

20. Beker, "Lessons from Martha Stewart on living well."

at a nearby Orthodox church and the pilgrims admired the beautiful icons in the worship space. Trying to get people back onto the bus from such a beautiful worship space felt more like trying to herd kittens. After several minutes of gentle cajoling and ushering people out of the space onto the bus, I realized we were one participant short. An elderly woman on the tour would not budge. She stood before an icon of our Savior and I assumed she was in a moment of deep devotion. As I neared the icon, however, I realized that this Eastern Orthodox depiction of Christ looked more like a body builder than a typical first-century Jewish carpenter. In fact, this Jesus was ripped with an impressive six-pack on the cross. "What are you thinking?" I asked the older woman as she stood there gazing. "Oh Pastor," she replied, "that's *my kind* of Savior." Yikes.

Missional leadership in today's global church requires a vibrant public witness without the benefits of wider cultural and political support that came with Christendom. Patrick writes his letter to the soldiers of Coroticus knowing full well that he has no authority or jurisdiction over him. He wrote the letter as a defiant, prophetic statement against the powers and principalities of his context, in light of the truth of the gospel.

While there are many threads of Patrick's ministry that speak to a passion for social justice, there is time and space to only profile only a few. To begin, Patrick's ministry empowered women in leadership in a way that was uncommon for the Hibernian society. Now, to be clear, this is not an attempt to somehow write a revisionist history of a fifth-century saint by proposing that St. Patrick was somehow a proto-feminist. No, we must see Patrick in the time and cultural context in which he gave his Christian witness, just as we should be judged in the future by the limitations and cultural prejudices of our time. Nevertheless, a mark of Patrick's social justice ministry was his defense of women and providing a place for those who wished to escape the cultural patriarchy of their time and its limitations on their freedom, through admission to a convent. Just as female leadership in the New Testament was a sign of the Holy Spirit's activity breaking down societal barriers, so too during Patrick's ministry women were early adopters to the gospel message. Patrick records this in his *Confession*

> How has this happened in Ireland? Never before did they know of God except to serve idols and unclean things. But now, they have become the people of the Lord, and are called children of God. The sons and daughters of the leaders of the Irish are seen to be monks and virgins of Christ! An example is this. There was a blessed Irish

woman of noble birth, a most beautiful adult whom I baptised. She came to us a few days later for this reason. She told us that she had received word from a messenger of God, who advised her that she should become a virgin of Christ, and that she should come close to God. Thanks be to God, six days later, enthusiastically and well, she took on the life that all virgins of God do. Their fathers don't like this, of course. These women suffer persecution and false accusations from their parents, and yet their number grows! We do not know the number of our people who were born there. In addition, there are the widows and the celibates. Of all these, those held in slavery work hardest—they bear even terror and threats, but the Lord gives grace to so many of the women who serve him. Even when it is forbidden, they bravely follow his example.[21]

It is interesting to note that Patrick does not use the word *pulchra* or beautiful but *pulcherrima* or surpassing beauty in describing the noblewoman whom he baptized.[22] As one scholar notes regarding the baptized noblewoman, "her presence . . . did not scare him or force him to denigrate, distort or demonise her bright feminine reality. She has a right to be Pulcherrima."[23] Patrick's ministry in Ireland was a source of liberation for many women who were moved from the patriarchal structure of Hibernian life to a less patriarchal society of the missionary church in something akin to the freedom women enjoyed in the early days of the church in the New Testament. Describing the noblewoman's choice, O'Donoghue argues, "in making her commitment to virginity and the search for divine union found herself part of a large and growing movement of dedicated women, not only young unwed women like herself but also widows and . . . married women who . . . had left their husbands."[24] Patrick's own understanding of family life beyond belonging to the family of God in the church is unclear. As William Swan surmises,

> There is no indication from the letters if Patrick was married with a family of his own but all the evidence points to the negative. The prevailing attitudes to sexuality were changing in the Western world around the fifth century with marriage and saintliness beginning to be seen as incompatible. Jerome saw marriage as being tied to the earth while those who dealt with heavenly things should

21. Patrick, *Confession*, Section 41 and 42.
22. O'Donoghue, *Aristocracy of the Soul*, 69.
23. Ibid., 72.
24. Ibid.

be celibate. With his quasi-monastic lifestyle in Hippo, Augustine set an example for fellow bishops just when monasticism was being taken as the ideal standard for Christian holiness. In both the *Confessio* and the *Epistola* Patrick mentions monks and virgins for the sake of the kingdom.[25]

Hearing Patrick's story reminds us sadly of how little has changed, for gender injustice and violence against woman continue in our time and place. Christians today must find our voice as Patrick did, to speak up and speak out against injustice from a minority stakeholder position in society. Surely, like Patrick, missional communities today are called to both create safe spaces for women and girls to live out their calling to Christ, as well as speak up and speak out against gender injustice in the broader community. Here in Cascadia I've been impressed by Abbotsford's own Sarah Bessey and author of *Jesus Feminist,* who describes herself as follows:

> I am one of those happy-clappy Jesus followers with stars in her eyes. I'm a Kingdom of God focused woman, postmodern, liberal to the conservative and conservative to the liberal in matters of both religion and politics (not an easy task, I assure you), a social justice wanna-be trying to do some good, and a nondenominational charismatic recovering know-it-all who has unexpectedly fallen back in love with the Church.[26]

Bessey's writing has a decidedly Cascadian, post-Christendom take on social justice. It's not the kind of fire off a petition to the politician or demand a seat at the table for negotiations approach that the mainline church thrived on while in Christendom. Instead, Bessey says that she wants to be outside the circles of power with the "misfits . . . rebels . . . dreamers . . . second-chance givers . . . radical grace lavishers . . . courageously vulnerable . . . and . . . especially the ones rejected by the Table as not worthy enough or right enough."[27] At the edges of power and the ends of the earth, a post-Christendom missional justice approach attends to "the work of justice and mercy, the glorious labor of reconciliation and redemption, the mess of friendship and community, the guts of walking on the water, and the big-sky dreaming of Kingdom of God."[28] That sounds like an approach to Christian witness that St. Patrick would admire.

25. Swan, *The Experience of God in the Writings of Saint Patrick,* 32.

26. http://sarahbessey.com/meet-sarah/.

27. Bessey, *Jesus Feminist,* 4.

28. Ibid.

Of course, from the letter to the soldiers of Coroticus, we see not only Patrick's concern for women but also for men and children, as he rails against the injustice of the slave trade. As a former slave himself, Patrick is enraged that people from a so-called "Christian society" would participate in such a barbaric practice. Of course, we often assume that human slavery is something in the past. Something that belongs to another century when William Wilberforce protested against slavery in the House of Commons or Abraham Lincoln signed the Emancipation Proclamation. But sadly slavery is alive and well in the world going under a new name—human trafficking. Our local Presbyterian church supports a ministry called Ratanak International, which attempts to address the challenge of poverty and the modern-day slave trade in Cambodia. The ministry was founded in Canada by Brian McConaghy, a now retired Royal Canadian Mounted Police forensics specialist who named the organization Ratanak, which means "precious gem" in Khmer, after he watched in a video as an eleven-month-old Cambodian baby named Ratanak died due to a lack of basic medical aid. McConaghy's Christian faith moved him to action in light of this injustice. McConaghy arranged for medical supplies and the building of hospitals and clinics. The care of orphans and abused children led to the provision of schools, building of orphanages and rehabilitation of children rescued from brothels. Ratanak also developed literacy, sanitation, and social services programs both in local communities and in prisons.

Ratanak International responds to the thousands of Cambodians who are trafficked and exploited, working to restore people robbed of freedom while protecting the vulnerable. Christians therefore continue to respond to the evil of slavery and sinful human trafficking with the same sense of moral outrage as Patrick had when calling out the injustice inflicted upon his converts long ago.

Patrick's ministry also shows signs of a deep love and care for creation. Just as we were careful not to project our twenty-first-century understanding of gender roles onto a fifth-century saint, so too should we not imagine St. Patrick as chasing after environmental polluters on a ship with Greenpeace in the Pacific Ocean waters of Cascadia. And yet, Celtic Christianity is marked by a deep reverence and respect for the gift of God's creation. As mentioned earlier, Patrick's slavery in Ireland and role as a shepherd placed him outdoors in all seasons. This daily connection with the ruggedness of the Irish climate proved to be the fertile ground for the Triune's God revelation.

After I arrived in Ireland, I tended sheep every day, and I prayed frequently during the day. More and more the love of God increased, and my sense of awe before God. Faith grew, and my spirit was moved, so that in one day I would pray up to one hundred times, and at night perhaps the same. I even remained in the woods and on the mountain, and I would rise to pray before dawn in snow and ice and rain. I never felt the worse for it, and I never felt lazy— as I realise now, the spirit was burning in me at that time.[29]

Patrick's discernment of God's faithful presence in the world helped spawn stories of Celtic saints who closely engaged the beauty, wonder, and power of creation in order to name the reality of the Creator. Apocryphal stories yoked to creation abound in Celtic Christianity, from Patrick using plant life to explain the Trinity, to Columba blessing a fruit tree to improve the sweetness of produce, to St. Brigid at the bedside of a dying chieftain in Kildare slowly weaving a cross from the rushes on the floor and explaining the meaning of the cross and Christ's atonement. The chieftain was so captivated by the story of Christ, as presented through the distinctive woven cross, that he requested baptism on his deathbed and died in peace. Creation remained for the Celtic Christians a wild, untamed reality that offered both risk and revelation. Take the classic depiction of God's activity in creation found in St. Patrick's Breastplate or the Lorica of St. Patrick:

> I arise today, through
> The strength of heaven,
> The light of the sun,
> The radiance of the moon,
> The splendor of fire,
> The speed of lightning,
> The swiftness of wind,
> The depth of the sea,
> The stability of the earth,
> The firmness of rock.

Environmental sensitivity and protection is a basic, widespread social norm in Cascadia today. While Cascadians would not view nature in the same way as their Hibernian counterparts, there is both a continuing sense of awe at creation's wild untamed nature and the possibility for

29. Patrick, *Confession*, 16.

revelation through it. Strolling along the beach in Tofino during storm season or waiting for a cancelled ferry in Tsawwassen during high winds or getting lost in the North Shore mountains or standing next to an enormous Douglas Fir tree that is 800 years old in Vancouver gives one a certain perspective about our relationship as creature to creation. So, too, in light of the Pacific Northwest's beauty, many would describe their encounter in creation as spiritual, if not going as far as to describe an awe for a creator. For Christians in Cascadia this cultural norm, care for creation, can become an obvious connection for our evangelistic witness and missional discipleship. Many churches organize cleanup projects and community gardens as ways of witnessing to our Christian care for God's creation and creatures. Creation becomes an apologetics laboratory where we can meet our pre-Christian neighbors in common love and care for the world with a shared sense of "general revelation." Whether one calls that general revelation shared with others prevenient grace like a Wesleyan or Common Grace like a Calvinist, there is a shared space in society for us to witness to the special revelation in God's covenant with Israel and the new covenant in the blood of Jesus Christ.

Finally, Patrick's ministry of proclamation and loving service to the people of Ireland contained the powerful gospel message of reconciliation and forgiveness that offered a different story to live in for the people of Hibernia. Ireland was a violent and harsh place in the fifth century. Clan fought clan and settling an argument by the sword was the acceptable social practice. Patrick's gospel announcement on behalf of Jesus Christ, the Prince of Peace, began to slowly shape the society over time. Indeed, a legend is told that Patrick came across two brothers engaged in a sword-fight over an inheritance dispute. The story goes that Patrick "froze" the two brothers in mid-fight and preached the gospel of peace to them. The brothers, suspended in mid-blows, listened carefully to the saint and when he released them they not only put away their swords but built a church on the spot in gratitude for their newfound life in Christ. It makes for a good story, but the reality of violence in our world today is just as real, and in fact, far greater in a world gripped by terror, haunted by the holocaust and other genocides, and in possession of more nuclear weapons than required to end life as we know it. From nuclear war on a global scale to domestic violence in our neighborhoods, we live in a violent world as in need of the Prince of Peace today as the people of Hibernia in Patrick's time.

Of course, modern-day Ireland has had its own share of violence and terror over the years. And yet, the modern day "Patrick's and Patricia's" continue to be called and equipped in the church to speak and live the gospel of peace. I've met some of those Irish peacemakers. One of our recent exchanges to Northern Ireland was to serve the good people of Fitzroy Presbyterian Church on the beautiful campus at Queen's University in Belfast. While staying in the manse with my family, I read the newly published memoirs of the previous minister, Rev. Ken Newell. Born into a strong evangelical Protestant family with deep Orange Lodge connections, his book traced his studies towards ordination, overseas missionary service in Indonesia, and softening viewpoints on the Catholic/Protestant divide in Ireland over the years. While serving Fitzroy Presbyterian Church for thirty years, he began a Bible study fellowship between his evangelical Presbyterian congregation and a local Roman Catholic Church. Ken notes that the quality time set aside for Bible study and prayer transformed relationships from "polite association to genuine friendship. When we tackled the obvious differences that existed among us, the respect we had cultivated at a spiritual level accelerated our acceptance of diversity as part and parcel of life."[30] At the time, at the height of the troubles, with shootings and bombings harming so many people on both sides of the conflict, this kind of "cross-community" action was unheard of and did not come without its fair share of risks. It was interesting sitting in the same manse in Belfast and reading about the late night phone calls and threats being made against the family for Ken's courageous leadership.

Ken's work, along with his Roman Catholic counterpart Father Gerry, was a sign of peace and a symbol of reconciliation. These servants of Christ were living out Paul's teaching

> Therefore, if anyone is in Christ, the new creation has come: The old has gone, the new is here! All this is from God, who reconciled us to himself through Christ and gave us the ministry of reconciliation: that God was reconciling the world to himself in Christ, not counting people's sins against them. And he has committed to us the message of reconciliation.[31]

The memoir's witness to the practice of reconciliation also shaped individuals and communities into a posture of righteousness. This was not just about being "nice" to those who were different or saying a quick "I'm

30. Newell, *Captured By a Vision*, 102.
31. 2 Cor 5: 18–19, *NIV.*

sorry" and moving on. No, this was about making a long-term commitment to relationship—a journey of Bible study, conversation, listening,
being present in the moments of discomfort and danger. Ken tells about
how this Bible study fellowship between Catholics and Protestants led to
joint Christmas carol services, shared public dialogue evenings between
the Catholic Archbishop and the Moderator of the Presbyterian Church in
Ireland—all while angry protesters (led by the infamous preacher and politician Ian Paisley) picketed outside and threatened violence.[32] But it was all
done with a purpose. It was a ministry of reconciliation that led to a deeper
love and appreciation of who Jesus Christ really is. When the relationship
between the two communities further developed, they began visiting sites
of violence and in the aftermath of a shooting or bombing the two communities held joint prayer vigils together as a sign of Christ's peace. Newell
served as Moderator of the Presbyterian Church in Ireland as well as the
chaplain to the first catholic Lord Mayor of Belfast. He understood that the
gospel of peace called him to cross borders, saying, "I'm like a shamrock.
Part of me is British, part of me is Irish and part of me is Ulster. I can move
between those easily. I value what's best in them all."[33] At the request of
the British Government, Newell and Father Gerry were involved in secret
discussions with Republican and Loyalist paramilitary groups that helped
contribute to the eventual Irish Republican Army and loyalist ceasefires of
1994. Newell and Father Gerry were awarded the Pax Christi International
Peace Prize for a grassroots reconciliation initiative in 1999.

The radical, risky commitment to peace and justice first brought to
Ireland by St. Patrick continues to empower and embolden followers of the
risen Christ today to speak up and speak out against injustice and violence
against creation and neighbor. This public witness does not require the
support or resources of our Christendom past. It requires missional communities of Christian faith who continue to read Scripture together, pray
and attend to both the brokenness in society and the reconciling love of the
Father, Son, and Holy Spirit at work around us.

A colleague of mine, Rev. Victor Kim of Richmond Presbyterian
Church, recently encountered anonymous racist flyers posted around the
community that has undergone massive ethnic and demographic shifts
in the last several decades. Reporter Douglas Todd describes Richmond
this way:

32. Newell, *Captured by a Vision*, 106.

33. Campbell, "Captured by a Vision."

a once-sleepy, semi-rural municipality suddenly turns into a buzzing city of more than 200,000 in which more than six out of 10 residents are born outside the country. No other city in Canada has a population in which 62 per cent of permanent residents are foreign born. It is rare for most global cities to contain even a fraction of non-nationals. In Mumbai and Shanghai, for instance, only one per cent of the population is foreign born.[34]

The racist posters produced by an "Alt Right" group against Chinese residents prompted Rev. Kim to organize an open letter in response with eighteen other churches and members of the wider multi-faith community. A protest was organized by Kim and picked up in the local media as a sign of faithful public witness.

Whether regarding gender injustice, human trafficking, abuse of the environment, violence at home or abroad or racism seeking to turn neighbor against neighbor, followers of the risen Christ today are in solidarity with those converts in Hibernia of old, praying in the worlds of St. Hilda:

> Have peace with each other as children of one mother
>
> let each defer to other and may your hearts be one.
>
> Have peace with all around you, sweet love of earth surround you
>
> and may no harm confront you or break the peace within.
>
> Have peace with God, your maker, in Jesus be partaker
>
> and Spirit consecrator, God, three in one, grant peace.
>
> The peace of God possess you, the love of God caress you,
>
> the grace of heaven bless you. Peace everlastingly.[35]

---

34. Todd, "Richmond."
35. Corrymeela Community's *Lenten Pilgrimage of Prayer for Peace*, 1.

CHAPTER 11

Croagh Patrick

Pilgrimage

*Christian life is a pilgrimage: it begins, continues,
and ends in God.*

—PRESBYTERIAN CHURCH IN CANADA, *LIVING FAITH 4.2.2*

"WE'RE STANDING ON HOLY ground," the woman said to her friend in a reverent tone. "I feel like I'm *on a pilgrimage*," she whispered, rubbing her debit card as if praying the rosary. I eavesdropped on this peculiar confession of faith during a recent day trip to Seattle. I was across the street from the Pike Place Market, picking up a coffee in a place that is, for some, a modern-day pilgrimage site: the first Starbucks coffee shop.

Pilgrimage is one of those curious words in our Christian lexicon that is part mysterious, part fussy, like *fellowship* or *narthex* or *tithing*. However, in a time when Western churches are keen to recover Christian practices in a quest to make post-Christendom disciples for Jesus, "pilgrimage" feels like a much-needed prodigal child coming home.

In her book *The Accidental Pilgrim*, Maggi Dawn explores our contemporary understanding of pilgrimage. Dawn, formerly of Cambridge, is now the Associate Dean of the chapel at Yale Divinity School, and writes in a beautiful style that feels like a warm knife through butter. She launches right into a reflection on her first visit to the Holy Land, a trip she made reluctantly, with a suitcase full of scepticism. While Dawn's visit to the troubled region was part of an academic tour, she couldn't help but notice the mixed motives and actions of pilgrims and tourists alike. Over time, she was transformed by the experience of pilgrimage, describing it as "a physical journey with a spiritual purpose."[1]

Returning home, Dawn continued to explore pilgrimage from Holy Island in the United Kingdom to the Black Madonna at Rocamadour in France. Her scholarly appetite led her through the Celtic tradition and left her wrestling with my own Reformed tradition's critique of religious journeying, recalling Martin Luther's firm stand in 1520: "All pilgrimages should be stopped. . . . These pilgrimages give countless occasions to commit sin and to despise God's commandments." John Calvin was equally put off by the notion of pilgrimage. Calvin was on alert for the clear and present danger that pilgrimage could so easily become a superstitious commercialization of devotion, whereby pilgrims could have the outward form of holiness but lack the "inward sentiment of devotion."[2] Calvin specifically listed pilgrimages as an example of faults contravening the Reformation, granting authorities "the right of chastising by means of prison or otherwise, or of punishing by extraordinary fines, at their discretion."[3] Calvin would likely agree with Peter Walker's contemporary critique of pilgrimage by arguing, "Jesus is the true holy site."[4]

And yet, as followers of Christ we celebrate the incarnation and the gift of our bodies not divorced from our souls in some Greek philosophical sense. Our embodiment as disciples brings with it opportunities to discover and celebrate new gifts from God within the covenant of grace. For Maggi Dawn, her appreciation for pilgrimage grew through the blessing and challenge of motherhood, and her discovery that "pilgrimage occurs despite imperfect circumstances and inconvenient timing."

In the end, Dawn stretches her understanding of pilgrimage, asking the reader to imagine a journey, not to a distant land, but within oneself. Confined to home for a summer by painful autoimmune arthritis, Dawn accepted the challenge to be an "armchair pilgrim" and to tend the soul through a journey of study and spirit. Her varied practices led her to an epiphany that "in the end, whether by accident or on purpose, it's not where you go but who you become that makes you a pilgrim."[5]

1. Dawn, *The Accidental Pilgrim*, 70.

2. Calvin, *Commentary on the Psalms 50:16.*

3. Quoted in Reid, *Calvin*, 80.

4. Quoted in Bartholomew, *Explorations in a Christian Theology of Pilgrimage*, 84.

5. Dawn, *The Accidental Pilgrim*, 147.

Pilgrimage is one way to describe St. Patrick's life story from Roman Britain to Hibernia, home to family and back again to minister in Ireland. Perhaps most importantly, Patrick's pilgrim story has inspired countless other disciples of Christ to make their own pilgrimage as a part of their spiritual discipline. Writing in 1920, Newport White observed, "It is undoubtedly true that Croagh-Patrick is the greatest Patrician sanctuary in Ireland. Antiquaries visit Slemish; but pilgrims in thousands climb Croagh-Patrick every year for the good of their souls."[6] Indeed, one of the most famous places associated with St. Patrick and pilgrimage *is* Croagh Patrick, outside the picture-perfect little town of Westport in County Mayo. I recall vacationing in Mayo a number of years ago with my wife and children as well as my cousins from Northern Ireland. Looming large in the distance above Westport is the mountain where legend says Patrick banished snakes following his great forty-day fast up Croagh Patrick. Once again, a story of Patrick belongs more to hagiography than to history. Snakes were not native to Ireland and likely the story has more to do with Patrick's battles with the Druids, whose symbol was a serpent. And yet, the story of Patrick's pilgrimage up the mountain in Mayo continues to inspire those who long to knit the temporal and spiritual together in order to experience a glimpse of the divine. Today, pilgrims gather at the end of July and make the 765-foot trek to the top of the mountain to show their piety—barefoot. Some of us (especially Reformed types like me) are more than happy to keep our hiking boots on while climbing Croagh Patrick and still arrive at the top of the mountain to stand face to face with the statue of the famous saint. It's curious standing there, looking at the saint's statue on that windswept hill since his image is so recognizable today around the world, but we don't really know what he looked like. The earliest identifiable image of St. Patrick comes to us in the year 1300 AD, although some have wondered whether a high cross at Kells in the ninth century depicts St. Patrick and St. Columba seated together.[7] And yet, as you climb the holy mountain in pilgrimage, that statute image of St. Patrick seems like just the right fit. The tradition goes back centuries as the journal of Count de Latocnaye notes in the 1790s:

> The mountain is called Croagh Patrick, and is a very celebrated place for the penitence of the faithful, who came from all parts on certain days of the year. They climb the mountain partly on their knees, or barefooted—I have been assured that on the fete day of

6. White, *St. Patrick*, 8.

7. MacShamhrain, ed., *The Island of St. Patrick*, 89.

the saint there may be so many as four or five thousand persons on the mountain.[8]

While many assume that the act of pilgrimage to Croagh Patrick was exclusively a Roman Catholic act, there is documented evidence that Protestants in Ireland also participated in the devotion. But what is it like to actually make the climb up the lonely mountain? In his classic 1930 work *In Search of Ireland*, H. V. Morton describes his own hike up Croagh Patrick:

> Patrick's Hill—lifts its magnificent cone 2,510 feet above the blue waters of Clew Bay. It is Ireland's Holy Mountain. The morning broke dangerously clear and fine. I took a stout stick and prepared to climb the mighty flank of Ireland's Sinai. As I approached it, admiring the high pattern of wheeling clouds over its head, I could see far off the little Mass chapel like a cairn of stones on the crest. . . .There is something terrifying, at least to me, in the mists that cover mountains—mists that hide you known not what; mists that cut a man off from the world and deny him the sight of the sky. To be lost on a mountain in mist is to experience all the horror of panic, for it seems to you that you might lose the path and go wandering vainly in circles answered only by a mocking laugh which seems to hide in all mountain mists. But I consoled myself by the thought that Croagh Patrick is a holy mountain from whose ravines and gullies all demons have been banished. Suddenly, right before me rose a white figure, and I looked up to a statue of St. Patrick.[9]

Morton's detailed account of climbing Croagh Patrick on pilgrimage puts flesh on the bones for what many experience as they embark on a journey of faith. Oliver St. John Gogarty, a contemporary of Morton's writing in the 1930s, describe reaching the top of Croagh Patrick with these words, "Suddenly Illumination! I had climbed Croagh Patrick. I had made the pilgrimage. I had become a worthy person through no fault of my own . . . .The Saint's strong soul was reigning influence still over all of us after fifteen hundred years."[10] Pilgrimage can be a transformative experience of God's revelation.

Over the years I have led pilgrimage tours to Ireland for church groups to walk in the footsteps of St. Patrick. I have also led several tours

8. McCormick, *Perceptions of St. Patrick in Eighteenth Century Ireland*, 36.

9. Morton, *In Search of Ireland*, 193.

10. St. John Gogarty, *I Follow St. Patrick*, 256.

to Israel/Palestine, Turkey, Greece, and Italy. These pilgrimage experiences have been a source of great blessing to many who describe their adult faith formation as taking giant steps forward in a short period of time, as they disconnect from their everyday lives in North America and focus on biblical sites or the stories of saints within a Christian community soaked in prayer, study, and praise. Wherever the destination for pilgrimage I often use the pilgrimage prayer from the Corrymeela Community in Ballycastle, Northern Ireland as a grounding for the steps of faith

> We started from different places.
>
> We share what ever we can.
>
> We journey together.
>
> Looking left and looking right for fellow pilgrims.
>
> Different, diverse but not divided.
>
> We journey together.
>
> We affirm this in the name of God
>
> who is at the end of the journey,
>
> The Christ who has gone before us
>
> And the Holy Spirit who accompanies us.

But just as Maggi Dawn discovered in her book *The Accidental Pilgrim*, the most challenging journey can be our own sanctification. Not a pilgrimage of place, but personhood. Not a journey marked by miles, but of maturity into the full measure of Christ. As Stephen Croft suggests, "The Church is [Jesus'] body, his bride, his pilgrim people travelling home to his eternal hope and rest."[11] In a sense, Patrick's gift of pilgrimage to us in a post-Christian context is an invitation to understand our walk with God in Christ in this one life as a pilgrimage from prodigal wandering to return to the gracious arms of the waiting Father. Or as the Corrymeela Community prayer in Northern Ireland says, "God who is at the end of the journey." Yes, "pilgrimage" feels like a much-needed homecoming for our prodigal child status to the Father who loves us more than we could ask or imagine. I've been reflecting lately on this gift in Scripture to us as Christians in post-Christendom whenever I read the pilgrimage of the prodigal home to the waiting Father in Luke 15.

One of the major pilgrimage places in the Middle Ages was Rome. I also have had the privilege of leading pilgrimage groups to sites in "the eternal

11. Croft, *Mission-Shaped Questions,* 198.

city." Of course, "when in Rome" one must also visit Vatican City, even for Protestants. If you've ever had the pleasure of visiting Vatican City no doubt you've spent time in the Sistine Chapel. It is a breathtaking space filled with some of Michelangelo's best work. As you crane your neck heavenward, however, there is this strange sensation as the crowd sweeps you through the chapel, the jostling, the cameras flashing, the muttering of excuse, excuse as you drift towards the other side of the room. Now there must be an off season for the Sistine Chapel but I haven't experienced it. As you desperately try to take it all in, you are fighting this sea of people rushing towards the exit like white water rafters in Cascadian rapids. You can imagine how easily one might lose a child or teenager in that space. It happened twice, in fact, to a former coworker of mine who was in Rome on vacation with her family. As Susan recalls the story, first Vivian her teenage daughter went missing for five minutes and was recovered nearby. She was soundly scolded and disciplined for her brief disappearance. Next, teenage Ben went missing in the sea of people and was nowhere to be found. Five minutes turned into ten and then into twenty and panic gripped Susan and her husband. They alerted Vatican security and as two hours clicked by were whisked through back alleys and corridors of the Vatican searching for Ben in something like you might see in *The Da Vinci Code* movie. Finally, Ben was found in St. Peter's Basilica and there was great rejoicing (something that would call for a robe, ring, and a feast). And everyone was happy. Everyone that is—except for Vivian. Vivian snorted, "So what, I got lost for five minutes and got into all kinds of trouble and my younger brother got lost for two hours and now he's the hero? Next time I'll get lost for longer."

Yes, there is a different perspective from a loving parent to rival siblings. And that is also visible in one of the most famous parables found in Scripture in Luke 15. The parable of the Prodigal Son has been called the most beautiful short story of all time. Rembrandt painted it, Kipling used it in poetry, the wider culture still gets the prodigal son references whether they have ever stepped inside a church or not. And what is this story?

Unlike Patrick's story of kidnapping and slavery we encounter the story of a young man who freely chooses to leave home. The story begins with a brash young man who is tired of life on the farm and wants to see the sights and sounds of the big city. He sizes his dad up and says with very little reverence, "Dad, you are healthy as a horse and I can't wait for you to die in order to receive my inheritance. So, why don't you give my portion of the inheritance today and I'll be off."

The father, for whatever reason, does divide his assets and gives the younger son what he is entitled to years before he should receive it. The son takes the inheritance, converts it into first-class airfare, travels to the far country, converts it into beer money, casino chips, and the coverage charge for the local gentlemen's club. Honesty, this guy appears to be having a good time. And what happens in the far country stays in the far country. If you know what I mean!

While in the far country, however, something funny happens over a period of time. The longer he goes living the good life, the more his inheritance shrinks and before you know it he is penniless. And now, you may find this surprising, but when the money dries up his friends disappear too. Imagine that! When the prodigal son stops buying all the rounds at the bar, he sits alone on the stool, nursing his Coke Zero until the owner tells him to get out. I guess the party's over. He gets a job, ironically on a local farm, just what he was trying to escape from in the first place—this time feeding pigs. Now, we don't necessarily get the sense of how low this guy has fallen. While we may enjoy a nice fry up of bacon and eggs in the morning (hopefully not every morning for the sake of your heart and arteries), pigs were unclean and forbidden animals to the folks who first heard this story in Jesus' day. Imagine as Jesus is teaching, one guy leans over to the other and says, "Wow, this guy in the story really *is* on hard times." This would be like Bill Gates, homeless, fishing through the garbage bins outside the Microsoft offices in Washington state. Hard times.

And then the prodigal "comes to his senses." The Bible says he thinks, "Why am I living like this when the hired help at my Dad's farm have good work, three square meals a day and a comfy bed to sleep in at night? I'm going home." Apparently not everything that happens in the far country, stays in the far country. Off he goes on his pilgrimage, and, unlike St. Patrick who trusted in a warm homecoming, the prodigal is slightly fearful about what kind of reception he is going to have on the farm. He starts practicing his speech on the way home . . . "Dad . . . I really screwed up . . ." "Dad, I know you're disappointed in me . . . I am too." "Father . . . I have sinned against heaven and before you; I am no longer worthy to be called your son; treat me like one of your hired servants."

While he's walking home and practicing his speech something the prodigal doesn't know, he couldn't know as a son, is that as a parent we see things differently. In fact, I imagine that everyday the father has been making a pilgrimage of his own, going to the edge of his property and looking down the long, winding road towards the far country . . . waiting, hoping, praying, even crying for his little guy to come home. Every day, the neighbor with his coffee and *Jerusalem Journal* newspaper in hand pulls back the curtains and looks out muttering, "Martha, there's that old fool looking for his son; that boy is never coming home." I imagine Patrick's parents looked out and longed for their lost son to return home every day as well as they scanned the horizon beyond Bannaventa Berniae.

The day the prodigal arrives home his father has gone out once more to the edge of the property to look with eyes of faith and a heart of fragile hope. Rubbing his eyes and fearing that his mind is playing tricks on him, the father sees his ragged, dirty, gaunt son staggering up the laneway. In those days, prominent men were never to run in public and yet, throwing public convention to the wind, the father picks up the edge of his robe and runs (showing his legs to all) down the laneway. The prodigal sees his dad coming and begins his speech, "Father, I have sinned . . ." but he gets no further before the old man wraps his arms around his son and they fall down to the ground together. The elderly man cradles his son in his arms just as he did when he was a baby. Tears of joy stream down the old man's face. The servants, worried about this crazy action of the father towards what they must assume is a beggar coming up the laneway, run to their Master's side. "Quickly, bring the best suit and finest bling I've got and put it on him, go and killed the best calf we've got and start a party—let's celebrate." The servants look at each other with surprise, wanting more answers. The old man smiles warmly, more than he has in years, and explains, "This is my son, who I thought was dead but is now alive!"

If Jesus had stopped the parable at this point, it would be a lovely story and we might all feel good and go on in our lives without any change. We might even search for a way to explain away the far country in a positive way . . . oh well, we all need to sow our wild oats, and so forth. Karl Barth even invoked this imagery of the far country in a positive way describing the incarnation of Jesus Christ as the Triune God's coming into the world as a redemptive journeying into the "far country." In other words, Jesus' birth, life, ministry, death, and resurrection takes place in the far country, our world rather than God's inner life.

While all very helpful, the story doesn't stop with the return of the prodigal, does it? No, as a Sunday school teacher once told me she was reviewing the prodigal son story and asking questions to see if the kids were absorbing the message. "Who goes away in this story?" the teacher asked.

"The prodigal son," one student replies. "And who welcomes the prodigal back with open arms?" the teacher continued. "The Father," says another. "And who is the one character who is upset at the prodigal's return?" asks the teacher. No answer. "Who must have been shocked at the way the day turned out?" tried the teacher again. No answer. "Um, name the character that has the most to lose?" said the teacher getting frustrated. One little kid put his hand up and said, "The fatted calf?"

I think the teacher was going more for the older brother. You know his story, don't you? The party is in full swing, the latest pop star is playing on the stereo, then the elder brother comes in from the fields, tired, dirty and ready for bed, when he hears the strangest sounds. Being senior management now on the farm, he snaps his fingers at one of the household servants, "What's this all about?" The servant looks nervous, "Um . . . ah . . . your little brother has come home and your dad has thrown a party complete with the fatted calf." The son immediately flies into a rage and throws farm tools this way and that before sitting down on the back porch. Soon after, alerted by the staff no doubt, the father comes out just as he came out to the prodigal earlier that day. The father invites the son into the party but the son refuses, saying, "I've always done everything you've asked and stayed here on the farm. You never throw a party like that for me but my brother, the total screw-up comes home and this is how you react?"

And we feel the anger, don't we? We feel the older brother's anger because many, many people here today are the older brother. While prodigals find a place within Christian communities I have always been struck by the response to this parable over the years coast to coast in North America. Shaking hands afterwards people usually lean in close and say, "I'm the older brother, what about him, pastor?" Now, I don't know what that says about church folks. Are we the responsible ones by and large, left to care for aging parents or ailing spouses, the ones who everyone can count on but who never receive the party with the fatted calf? Are you still waiting for *your* fatted calf?

Perhaps your Christian community is more of an elder brother or sister congregation than a prodigal child church? The danger of course is the picture of that elder brother stewing on the back porch, his dad's arm around him trying to comfort him while he is just seething with anger. If you scratch just a little bit below the surface of his "duty speech" ("all I've ever done is work this land") you'll find self-righteous indignation and a lack of forgiveness that is eating him up from the inside. Surely, that's not how God intends us to live as fully alive, fully redeemed human beings. Surely that's not the path of pilgrimage that God intends for us. Now, I'm not saying that as the responsible one, the elder brother or elder sister, we should be happy about the shenanigans of the prodigals in our family and our lives. What I am saying is that we need to be careful that in our anger we do not overlook or minimize the incredible blessings that God has giving us in that caring role.

My Uncle Ken was the prodigal in our family life growing up. The care of my lovely, aging grandmother fell squarely on my mother's shoulders. Although Ken had extracted his own "prodigal son equivalent" from my grandfather's successful business over the years in order to sow his wild oats in the far country, he was nowhere to be seen as my grandma's health declined. Perhaps not surprisingly, however, at the last minute he appeared by the bedside in the hospital. It was almost time to read the will and I suppose he wanted to make sure he wasn't cut out for bad behavior. After he left, my grandmother said to my Mom, "I know all that you've done for me and I appreciated it so much, you are a good daughter. But I am dividing the estate 50/50. He's still my son." While that truth stung a little, I still remember my mom saying that the greatest gift or inheritance she had was simply those years with my grandmother that her brother missed out on. I thought of that the day of the funeral when I saw my Uncle parading around accepting half-baked condolences from family and friends, collecting his check and then moving on and out of our lives never to be seen again.

No, the prodigal may seem to win at first glance but in fact, he loses out in so many other ways. The law was clear in Jesus' day: the elder brother stewing on the back porch had already received his inheritance. Ironically, the prodigal's rude demand for inheritance has made the older brother rich. You see, in that day the eldest sibling inherited what was called a "double portion," the greater part of the family wealth with the understanding that he would take over the farm, care for the parents in old age, and represent the family in the wider community.[12] The prodigal received one-third of the value of the farm and wasted it. The brother received two-thirds of the farm and became the boss.

So, the elder brother did receive his inheritance, in fact a double portion. The next day, the prodigal would get up, his head ringing a little with a hangover from the party the night before, and discover that now he was an employee and at the mercy of that older brother. What would happen

12. Deut 21:15–17.

then? What might a pilgrimage for the two brothers together look like? Jesus deliberately stops short of saying—for here is where our work begins. We are drawn so deeply into this incredible story of pilgrimage either as the reckless prodigal or responsible older brother. We cannot help but read this parable through the lens of our own life and family experiences as the gospel shines a light on those dark areas of our lives that we prefer not to look at behind our Sunday best.

While it may undermine our desire for fairness, the reality from this parable is that God as our loving Father runs to greet the prodigal who returns and sits patiently with arm around the elder brother loving him into the party. This is the warmth of the God that encountered a scared and lonely teenager named Patrick on Slemish mountain and began his pilgrimage to sainthood. The prodigal makes the pilgrimage home over many miles but the older brother's pilgrimage must take him even further—the distance between his head and his heart. Whether like the prodigal we feel we are not worthy of God's love, or whether like the elder brother we have convinced ourselves that we've earned God's love—in the end both are wrong. As prodigals and as elder siblings God's grace and God's love finds us and accepts just for who we are. What a strange, unsettling, and wonderful God we worship. Wherever you are in your pilgrimage whether

on the laneway,

or the back porch,

isn't it time to come inside,

isn't it time to come home?

CHAPTER 12

Downpatrick

An End and New Beginning

*"You will be my witnesses in Jerusalem, and in all Judea,
and Samaria, and to the ends of the earth."*

—ACTS 1:8B

SEVERAL YEARS AGO I found myself with a green beer in hand, standing on the streets of the small town of Downpatrick on a rather drizzly yet festive March 17. Downpatrick is a short five-minute drive from Saul, where Patrick began his ministry in Ireland. As I stood with friends watching the colorful St. Patrick's Day parade go by and sipping a wee green-tinted Harp lager, a man quietly walked through the crowd handing out small cards to the people on the sidelines. While some may think the legacy of Patrick is limited to boisterous parties and green beer on March 17, this humble man, this quiet witness to the gospel of Jesus, made his way through the crowd smiling politely and passing out the small gift to anyone who would take it. I smiled back at the man and thanked him as he placed a card in my hand with the same gentleness and reverence that a priest might place a communion wafer. I looked down at the card and read these words attributed to St. Patrick:

> Christ be with me, Christ within me.
> Christ behind me, Christ before me.
> Christ beside me, Christ to win me.
> Christ to comfort and restore me.

Christ beneath me, Christ above me

Christ in quiet, Christ in danger.

Christ in hearts of those who love me.

Christ in mouth of friend and stranger.

As the crowd roared in approval of the floats passing by, and green beer spilled on the cobblestones around me, I was transfixed by the small, dignified witness this man made in the midst of the lively street party. I read the words again slowly and I was struck by the beauty and power of this faithful act that surely would have warmed Patrick's heart far more than the shamrock hats or cartoon saints and snakes t-shirts parading around me. I looked up to say a word of thanks to the shy evangelist—but he was gone.

What we know of Patrick's ending is that by March 461 AD, the old missionary bishop was in poor health and nearing the end of his earthly days. According to tradition, an angel announced to Patrick that his death would be soon and so he "leaves Saul for his beloved city of Armagh, but out of a bush burning by the roadside the angel Victor bids him return to Saul, where he is to die; he obeys and is told that he has been granted four requests, including a place of special honor for Armagh."[1] Patrick died at Saul thus marking the end of his ministry in the same place where it had its new beginning long ago with his first convert and church plant. By the end of Patrick's life, Hibernia was more peaceful and civilized just as the Roman world was heading in the opposite direction. Thomas Cahill surmises, "As the Roman lands went from peace to chaos, the land of Ireland was rushing ever more rapidly from chaos to peace."[2] The change in the state of the church and the power of Christian witness in Patrick's lifetime is hard to overstate. Of course, some have tried including the author of *The Annals of the Four Masters,* who records Patrick's death on March 17, 461 AD in this way:

> Patrick . . . archbishop, first primate, and chief apostle of Ireland . . . was the person who separated them from the worship of idols and spectre . . . and brought them from the darkness of sin and vice to the light of faith and good works, and who guided and conducted their souls from the gates of hell (to which they were going), to the gates of the kingdom of heaven. It was he that baptized and blessed the men, women, sons and daughters of Ireland,

1. Bieler, *The Patrician Texts in the Book of Armagh,* 8. It's good to know that with the burning bush at the end of Patrick's life we can confirm he was clearly a good Presbyterian!

2. Cahill, *How the Irish Saved Civilization,* 122.

with their territories and tribes, both fresh waters and sea inlets. It was by him that many cells, monasteries, and churches were erected throughout Ireland; seven hundred churches was their number. It was by him that bishops, priests, and persons of every dignity were ordained; seven hundred bishops, and three thousand priests was their number. He worked so many miracles and wonders, that the human mind is incapable of remembering or recording the amount of good which he did upon earth. When the time of St. Patrick's death approached, he received the Body of Christ from the hands of the holy Bishop Tassach . . . and resigned his spirit to heaven.[3]

While contemporary obituaries are full of hyperbole and unfounded praise thick enough to make any sinner appear as a saint, *The Annals of the Four Masters* may go so far as to make any humble servant of Christ like Patrick blush and look over his or her shoulder to see who we are really talking about. A more recent and measured assessment is offered by Jonathan Rogers, who reviews Patrick's ministry and suggests that the achievements of the historical Patrick were no less miraculous than those of the legendary Patrick. Perhaps the most miraculous thing of all, according to Rogers, was that even as he brought the gospel of Christ to bear on the Irish, Patrick left their Irishness intact. The Irish didn't have to become Roman in order to become Christian and as Rogers concludes, "that may seem obvious from where we sit, but it wasn't at all obvious in Patrick's time. His was a renewed vision of what it means to be a follower of Christ: just as the apostle Paul brought Christianity out from under the umbrella of Jewish culture, Patrick demonstrated that Christianity was bigger than the Roman Empire."[4]

As Christians living in the twenty-first century West, we too exercise our discipleship in a context that requires us to translate the gospel through a new form of witness. As the church grapples with its Christendom legacy in a post-Christendom world, we can learn much from the missionary bishop to Hibernia who proclaimed Jesus Christ, crucified and risen, in a way that was free from the cultural demands of the Roman Empire. In this book we have followed the footsteps of Patricius from his early childhood through captivity and conversion through his calling and equipping to the missionary life. We have watched with wonder as he courageously preached and lived the gospel of Christ amongst a challenging and, at times, hostile community of people Jesus died to save. Could the young shepherd slave

3. O'Donovan, *Annals of the Kingdom of Ireland by the Four Masters*, 66.

4. Rogers, *St Patrick*, xv.

praying a hundred times a day and a hundred times at night ever imagine the legacy we enjoy today from his ministry? Surely not! Therefore, that should give us encouragement as we go about our own humble and passionate witness to Jesus. We follow in the footsteps of Patrick by witnessing in our own challenging and, at times, hostile context, by proclaiming the life-saving, world-changing action of the Triune God through the cradle and empty cross of Christ. Patrick's story gives us encouragement to share and live the gospel with urgency in the mission field God has appointed us to in our everyday ordinary lives within our homes, workplaces, churches and the communities where we live, work and play.

Setting my green beer aside, I clutched the wee card from the shy evangelist imprinted with St. Patrick's bold witness and followed the parade up the street towards Down Cathedral. *Christ behind me. Christ before me.* Leaving the parade route, I walked up the steep pathway towards the Cathedral transforming a little with every step from partygoer to pilgrim. *Christ beside me, Christ to win me.* I walked past the large stone that marks the traditional burial site of our Saint, his name and a simple Celtic cross chiseled on top. *Christ beneath me, Christ above me.* Reaching the door of the Cathedral, I was warmly greeted by an usher who welcomed me into the worship space as the sound of voices raised in song filled my ears and stirred my soul. *Christ in hearts of those who love me.* I slid into a back pew, still gingerly holding the card with St. Patrick's words like a Presbyterian communion token required in years gone by, and looked off the open hymnbook of the woman beside me. *Christ in mouth of friend and stranger.*

Local Catholic and Protestant churches were participating in an ecumenical service and together the people were singing the old hymn "St. Patrick's Breastplate." The congregation sang with a flourish of trumpets and thundering organ, "I bind this day to me forever, by power of faith, Christ's incarnation, his baptism in the Jordan river, his death on cross for my salvation, his busting from the spiced tomb, his riding up the heavenly way, his coming at the day of doom, I bind unto myself today." With a party in the street and praise in the Cathedral, Patrick's ongoing impact on the people of Hibernia felt undeniable. The congregation continued to lift up their voices to the Triune God in another verse extolling, with a nod to John Calvin, creation as the theatre of God's glory, singing of "the virtues of the starlit heaven . . . the flashing of the lightning free." We sang of God's providential care of creation and its creatures with "God's eye to watch, God's might to stay . . . God's hand to guide, God's shield to ward." And then, in the fifth verse the whole hymn shifted tone from a triumphalist declaration of God's power to something more like a whisper of confession as the congregation sang the words that I received on the street and that led me to this holy place. *Christ be with me, Christ within me. Christ in quiet, Christ in danger. Christ to comfort and restore me.* As I surveyed the worship space overflowing with Christians of all denominations, I was touched once more by the impact of a frightened and faithful teenager's "yes" to God's comforting and commanding presence on Slemish mountain long ago. I was reminded of God's surprising gift of revelation and call from generation to generation. Standing at Downpatrick reminded me once more that where we see dead endings God sees new beginnings, promises and possibilities beyond our imagination. Indeed, every Advent we tell another story of a frightened and faithful teenager's "yes" in Nazareth long ago that changed the world forever. This same God continues to call ordinary, fragile, fallible human beings like you and me, breathing new life and hope into this fallen world as we await the completion of God the Father's reconciling and redeeming work in Jesus Christ through the Holy Spirit. *Let it be with us, according to thy Word.*

Our missional task is no more daunting that the one facing Patrick as he stepped ashore in Hibernia and began his ministry in Saul. Today, we too are tasked with Christian witness in a sinsick and skeptical world. Like Patrick's arrival as a missionary on the shores of Hibernia, we offer *our* Christian witness in light of what God is *already doing in the world.* As Lesslie Newbigin reminds us, "Our gospel is not the thoughts of (people) but the acts of God."[5] Our waymaker God is active in creation, redeeming and reconciling the cosmos in the resurrected Christ through the power of the Holy Spirit. Like Patrick, our calling is to boldly proclaim this eternal truth through the limitations of our sinful, temporal human frame, trusting that God will receive our fragile gift with grace, as with a child bringing a haphazard painting or muddled craftwork with pride to his or her loving parent. Engagement in Christian witness through a missional community requires a longing to be set free from our Christendom past as well as a desire for the Triune God to disempower our depravity and enliven us by his grace. We engage in this missional work in the twenty-first century West as Patrick did in his own fifth-century Hibernia—not by relying on our own strength but on God's power alone. We bind ourselves to the strong name of the Trinity and pray for the courage and commitment to witness to God's grace and goodness

---

5. Newbigin, *Sin and Salvation*, 43.

in our lives and the world around us until the kingdom comes. God gave me a glimpse of the heavenly banquet that day in Down Cathedral. Invited into a feast not of my own design or choosing by the humble witness of a shy evangelist. Welcomed warmly by strangers who revealed themselves to be kin, by adoption, in the family of God. In worship the body of Christ, in all its beautiful diversity, sang of the One who holds us together, of the One who holds us dear. We sang with Patrick's witness to the Triune God who is always out ahead of us, working to make all things new. I stood in the Cathedral that St. Patrick's Day overwhelmed by joy and delight, speechless as the congregation continued to sing for me, "I bind unto myself the name, the strong name of the Trinity, by invocation of the same, the Three in One and One in Three, of whom all nature has creation, eternal Father, Spirit, Word. Praise to the Lord of my salvation; salvation is of Christ the Lord." Patrick's ministry ended at Saul and Downpatrick long ago, just as our ministries will surely end one day when we no longer have breath to sing God's praise. But until the day of consummation, God will continue to raise up after us missionary disciples for the sake of witness, just as God has always done, to sing the songs of praise when our lips are sealed. When we can no longer sing heaven's song on earth, by grace, we will cheer others on from the communion of Saints as new missionary disciples worship, work, and witness in order to point others towards the joy of the gospel which is life in communion with God: Father, Son, and Holy Spirit.

For now, Patrick's ministry to a pre-Christian people continues to inspire our own Christian witness as we discern what it means to be the church in the ruins of Christendom. Just as Patrick's death was a new beginning for the Irish Church, we also look forward in hope to the shape and content of new, faithful Christian witness in a cultural landscape that God is out ahead of us creating. Whatever that witness may look like, we trust that the One, who went ahead of the people of Israel a pillar of cloud by day and a pillar of fire by night, goes ahead of the church in our time and place. It is said that Patrick believed his ministry would be complete when every person in Ireland had two phrases upon their lips—*Kyrie Eleison* and *Deo Gratias*.

As we worship, work and witness to the power of the gospel and the resurrection of our Lord Jesus Christ here in Cascadia and beyond, may those who encounter us as his missionary disciples, saved to be sent, always have on our lips:

Lord, have mercy. Thanks be to God.

Discussion Questions

for individual reflection or
small group discussion

Chapter One: Bannaventa Berniae

- How has the church in society changed since your childhood—what would you count as gain or loss?

- Who first taught you the Christian faith? How did their teaching and lifestyle shape your living?

Chapter Two: Slemish

- When did your faith in God become real? What happened and who did you tell?

- How has God used adversity to shape your discipleship?

Chapter Three: Uillula

- What does the idea of being "homesick at home" mean to you?

- Recall a story of homecoming in your own life story. Who was there? How did they respond? What had changed since you left?

Chapter Four: Auxerre

- What is the most significant thing God has taught you in the last year?

- If you had unlimited time and resources, what's one course of study you would love to enroll in? What would you like to learn and why?

Chapter Five: Saul

- Tell a story about a time in your life when you started something new. What did you learn about yourself in the process?

- If you could start a new church what you do? What would you keep from your old church? What new ideas or practices would you introduce?

Chapter Six: Slane

- Where have you encountered resistance to sharing the gospel in your own context? What did you do to overcome or work around that resistance?

- If there is a force at work in the world that would do us harm, how does that shape our faithful witness as Christians?

Chapter Seven: Cashel

- If you could introduce someone to Jesus what would you say about him to others? What does abundant life in Jesus look like in the world? What does it look like in your life?

- What are some of the stumbling blocks to people converting to Christianity today in your context?

Chapter Eight: Armagh

- What is the most comforting or challenging part of the way your current Christian community is structured? How might that structure be reformed to free people up for mission?

- What is the purpose(s) for having any structure to a Christian community beyond the local congregation?

Chapter Nine: Monasterboice

- If you were to share daily life in community with other Christians, what "rules" would you expect to live by?

- How are you accountable to others in your discipleship to Jesus?

Chapter Ten: Ail

- When have you been outraged by injustice enough to speak up and speak out about it?

- What examples of injustice are currently taking place in the world that must surely break God's heart?

Chapter Eleven: Croagh Patrick

- What words or images best describe your journey of faith so far with Jesus?

- What is your next most faithful step in this pilgrimage through life with God?

Chapter Twelve: Downpatrick

- What hope and strength does the promise of resurrection offer for life before death as well as life beyond death?

- What would you hope to be remembered for?

Further Reading

Airhart, Phyllis. *The Church with the Soul of a Nation*. Montreal/Kingston: McGill-Queen's University Press, 2014.

Barth, Karl. *Church Dogmatics*. Peabody, MA: Hendrickson, 2010.

———. *Deliverance to the Captives*. Toronto: Fitzhenry and Whiteside, 1978.

Bartholomew, Craig. *Explorations in a Christian Theology of Pilgrimage*. Burlington, VT: Ashgate, 2004.

Beach, Lee. *The Church in Exile: Living in Hope After Christendom*. Downer's Grove, IL: Intervarsity, 2015.

Beker, Jeanne. "Lessons from Martha Stewart on living well: 'We don't preach. We teach.'" *The Globe and Mail*, October 19, 2016.

Bessey, Sarah. *Jesus Feminist: An Invitation to Revisit the Bible's View of Women*. New York: Howard, 2013.

Bieler, Ludwig. *The Patrician Texts in the Book of Armagh*. Oxford: Oxford University Press, 1979.

———. *The Works of St. Patrick*. London: The Newman Press, 1953.

Block, Tina. *The Secular Northwest: Religion and Irreligion in Everyday Postwar Life*. Vancouver, BC: University of British Columbia Press, 2016.

Bosch, David. *Transforming Mission: Paradigm Shifts in Theology of Mission*. Maryknoll: Orbis, 1991.

Brueggemann, Walter. *Biblical Perspectives on Evangelism: Living in a Three-Storied Universe*. Nashville: Abingdon, 1993.

Byassee, Jason, and John M. Buchanan, eds. *From the Editor's Desk: Thinking Critically, Living Faithfully at the Dawn of a New Christian Century*. Louisville: Westminster/John Knox, 2016.

Cahill, Thomas. *How the Irish Saved Civilization*. New York: Anchor, 1996.

Calvin, John. *Commentaries on the Epistles to Timothy, Titus, and Philemon*. Translated by William Pringle. Grand Rapids: Baker, 1979.

———. *Commentary on the Book of Psalms*. Edinburgh: Printed for the Calvin Translation Society, 1845.

Campbell, Brian. "Captured by a Vision." *Irish Times*, May 21, 2016.

Charles-Edwards, Thomas. *St. Patrick and the Landscape of Early Christian Ireland*. The 2011 Kathleen Hughes Memorial Lectures. Cambridge: Cambridge University Press, 2012.

Charry, Ellen. *By The Renewing of Your Minds: The Pastoral Function of Christian Doctrine.* Oxford: Oxford University Press, 1997.

Chilcote, Paul, ed. *The Study of Evangelism: Exploring a Missional Practice of the Church.* Grand Rapids: Eerdmans, 2008.

Conneely, Daniel. *St. Patrick's Letters: A Study of their Theological Dimension.* Maynooth: An Sagart, 1993.

Corrymeela Community. *Lenten Pilgrimage of Prayer for Peace.* https://www.corrymeela. org/emsfiles/events/2016/2Feb2016/Lenten-Walks-2016-CORRYMEELA.pdf.

Crofford, Gregory. *Mere Ecclesiology: Finding Your Place in the Church's Mission.* Eugene, OR: Wipf & Stock, 2016.

Croft, Stephen. *Mission-Shaped Questions: Defining Issues for Today's Church.* London: Church House, 2008.

Cronshaw, Darren, and Kim Hammond. *Sentness: Six Postures of Missional Christians.* Downer's Grove, IL: Intervarsity, 2014.

Cusack, M. F. *The Life of St. Patrick: Apostle of Ireland.* London: Longmans, Green and Co. 1871.

Dawn, Maggi. *The Accidental Pilgrim: New Journeys on Ancient Pathways.* London: Hodder and Stoughton, 2011.

De Breffny, Brian. *In the Steps of St. Patrick.* London: Thames and Hudson, 1982.

de Paor, Maire. *Patrick the Pilgrim Apostle of Ireland.* Dublin: Veritas, 1998.

Duckworth, Jessica. *Wide Welcome: How the Unsettling Presence of Newcomers Can Save the Church.* Minneapolis: Fortress, 2013.

Dulles, Avery. *Models of the Church.* New York: Image, 1974.

Dumville, David. *St. Patrick.* Suffolk: Boydell, 1993.

Fitch, David. *Faithful Presence: Seven Disciplines that Shape the Church for Mission.* Downer's Grove, IL: Intervarsity, 2016.

Francis. *Evangelii Gaudium: Apostolic Exhortation on the Proclamation of the Gospel in Today's World.* Vatican, November 24, 2013.

Freeman, Philip. *St. Patrick of Ireland: A Biography.* New York: Simon & Schuster, 2004.

———. *The World of Saint Patrick.* Oxford: Oxford University Press, 2014.

Frost, Michael. *Exiles: Living Missionally in a Post-Christian Culture.* Peabody, MA: Hendrickson, 2006.

Frost, Michael, and Alan Hirsch, *The Faith of Leap: Embracing a Theology of Risk, Adventure and Courage.* Grand Rapids: Baker, 2011.

General Synod of the Dutch Reformed Church. *The Framework Document on the Missional Nature and Calling of the Dutch Reformed Church,* 2013. http://www.academia. edu/9789282/FRAMEWORK_DOCUMENT_ON_THE_MISSIONAL_NATURE_ AND_CALLING_OF_THE_DUTCH_REFORMED_CHURCH.

Goheen, Michael W., ed. *Reading the Bible Missionally.* Grand Rapids: Eerdmans, 2016.

Greenman, Jeffrey. *Pedagogy of Praise: How Congregational Worship Shapes Christian Character.* Vancouver: Regent College, 2016.

Guder, Darrell. *The Incarnation and the Church's Witness.* Eugene, OR: Wipf and Stock, 2005.

Guder, Darrell, ed. *Missional Church: A Vision for the Sending of the Church in North America.* Grand Rapids: Eerdmans, 1998.

Hall, Douglas John. *Why Christian? For Those on the Edge of Faith.* Minneapolis: Fortress, 1998.

Hanson, R. P. C. *The Life and Writings of the Historical Saint Patrick*. New York: Seabury, 1983.

Haokip, Jangkholam, and K. Sungjemmeren Imchen, eds. *Becoming a Missional Congregation in the Twenty-First Indian Context*. Delhi: Kaba/CMS-UBS, 2016.

Hastings, Ross. *Missional God, Missional Church: Hope for Re-Evangelizing the West*. Downers Grove, IL: Intervarsity, 2012.

Herbenick, Raymond M. *On the Erudition of the Historical St. Patrick*. Lewiston, NJ: Edwin Mellen, 2000.

Hirsch, Alan. *The Forgotten Ways: Reactivating Apostolic Movements*. 2d ed. Grand Rapids: Brazos, 2016.

Hitchcock, F. R. Montgomery. *St. Patrick and His Gallic Friends*. London: SPCK, 1916.

Hopkin, Alannah. *The Living Legend of St. Patrick*. New York: St. Martin's, 1989.

Howlett, D. R. *The Book of Letters of Saint Patrick the Bishop*. Dublin: Four Court, 1994.

Keum, Jooseop, ed. *Together towards Life: Mission and Evangelism in Changing Landscapes—with a Practical Guide*. Geneva: WCC, 2013.

Labberton, Mark. *Called: The Crisis and Promise of Following Jesus Today*. Downer's Grove, IL: Intervarsity, 2014.

Lewis, C. S. *Collected Letters, Volumes 1 and 2*. San Francisco: Harper, 2005.

Lockhart, Ross A. *Lessons from Laodicea: Missional Leadership in a Culture of Affluence*. Eugene, OR: Cascade, 2016.

Longley, Michael, and Frank Ormsby, eds. *The Selected Poems of John Hewitt*. Belfast: Blackstaff, 2007.

MacShamhrain, Ailbhe, ed. *The Island of St. Patrick: Church and Ruling Dynasties in Fingal and Meath, 400–1148*. Dublin: Four Court, 2004.

McCormack, Jim. *St. Patrick: The Real Story as Told in His Own Words*. Dublin: Columba, 2008.

McCormick, Bridget. *Perceptions of St. Patrick in Eighteenth Century Ireland*. Dublin: Four Court, 2000.

McNeal, Reggie. *Missional Renaissance: Changing the Scorecard for the Church*. San Francisco: Jossey Bass, 2009.

Miller, Calvin. *Celtic Devotions: A Guide to Morning and Evening Prayer*. Downer's Grove, IL: Intervarsity, 2013.

Morton, H. V. *In Search of Ireland*. London: Methuen, 1930.

Newbigin, Lesslie. *The Gospel in a Pluralist Society*. Grand Rapids: Eerdmans, 1989.

———. *The Open Secret: An Introduction to the Theology of Mission*. Grand Rapids: Eerdmans, 1995.

———. *Sin and Salvation*. Eugene, OR: Wipf and Stock, 2009.

Newell, Ken. *Captured By A Vision: A Memoir*. Newtownards: Colourpoint, 2016.

O'Donoghue, Noel Dermot. *Aristocracy of Soul: Patrick of Ireland*. Wilmington: Michael Glazer, 1987.

O'Donovan, John. *Annals of the Kingdom of Ireland by the Four Masters*. Dublin: Hodges and Smith, 1851.

O'Loughlin, Thomas. *Discovering Saint Patrick*. New York: Paulist, 2005.

———. *Saint Patrick: The Man and His Works*. London: Triangle/SPCK, 1999.

Osmer, Richard. *Practical Theology: An Introduction*. Grand Rapids: Eerdmans, 2008.

Osmer, Richard, and Friedrich Schweitzer. *Religious Education between Modernization and Globalization*. Grand Rapids: Eerdmans, 2003.

Paas, Stephan. *Church Planting in the Secular West: Learning from the European Experience.* Grand Rapids, Eerdmans, 2016.

Patrick, *Confessio and Epistola.* Translated by Padraig McCarthy, 2003. www.confessio.ie.

Paulsen, Judy. *Christian Foundations: A Grounding for a life of Faith.* Toronto: Wycliffe College, 2016.

Peterson, Eugene. *Five Smooth Stones for Pastoral Work.* Grand Rapids: Eerdmans, 1992.

The Presbyterian Church in Canada. *Living Faith/Foi Vivante: A Statement of Christian Belief.* Winfield: Wood Lake, 1984.

Purves, Andrew. *Crucifixion of Ministry.* Downer's Grove, IL: Intervarsity, 2007.

———. *Reconstructing Pastoral Theology: A Christological Foundation.* Louisville: Westminster John Knox, 2004.

Reid, J. K. S. *Calvin: Theological Treatises.* London: SCM, 1954.

Rogers, Jonathan. *St Patrick.* Nashville: Thomas Nelson, 2010.

Root, Andrew. *The Promise of Despair: The Way of the Cross as the Way of the Church.* Nashville: Abingdon, 2010.

Roxburgh, Allan. *Structured for Mission.* Downer's Grove, IL: Intervarsity, 2015.

Roxburgh, Allan J., and M. Scott Boren. *Introducing the Missional Church: What It is, Why It matters, How to Become One.* Grand Rapids: Baker, 2009.

Schleiermacher, Friedrich. *On Religion: Speeches to its Cultured Despisers.* Translated by Richard Crouter. Cambridge: Cambridge University Press, 1996.

Sparks, Paul, Tim Soerens, and Dwight Friesen, eds. *The New Parish: How Neighborhood Churches are Transforming Mission, Discipleship and Community.* Downers Grove, IL: Intervarsity, 2014.

St. John Gogarty, Oliver. *I Follow St. Patrick.* London: Rich and Cowan, 1938.

Stone, Bryan. *Evangelism After Christendom: The Theology and Practice of Christian Witness.* Grand Rapids: Brazos, 2007.

Swan, William. *The Experience of God in the Writings of Saint Patrick: Reworking A Faith Received.* Rome: Pontifical Biblical Institute, 2013.

Sweet, Leonard. *The Gospel According to Starbucks: Living with a Grande Passion.* Colorado Springs, CO: WaterBrook, 2007.

Swift, Edmund. *The Life and Acts of Saint Patrick: A Translation from the Original Latin of Jocelin of Furnes.* Dublin: Hibernia, 1809.

Taylor, Charles. *A Secular Age.* Harvard, MA: The Belknap Press of Harvard University Press, 2007.

Thompson, E. A. *Who Was St. Patrick?* Suffolk: Boydell, 1985.

Todd, Douglas. *Cascadia: The Elusive Utopia.* Vancouver: Ronsdale, 2008.

———. "Richmond: Global Centre of a Demographic Explosion." *The Vancouver Sun,* June 16, 2015.

Topping, Richard. "Troubling Context: Mainline Theological Education and Formation in Canada." *Encounter* 76.3 (2016) 39–54.

Torrance, David W., and Thomas F. Torrance, eds. *Calvin's Commentaries.* Grand Rapids: Eerdmans, 1966.

Torrance, James. B. *Worship, Community and the Triune God of Grace.* Downer's Grove, IL: Intervarsity, 1997.

Torrance, Thomas. *Reality and Evangelical Theology: The Realism of Christian Revelation.* Downers Grove, IL: Intervarsity, 1982.

Truth and Reconciliation Canada. *Honouring the Truth, Reconciling for the Future: Summary of the Final Report of the Truth and Reconciliation Commission of Canada.* Winnipeg: Truth and Reconciliation Commission of Canada, 2015.

Van Gelder, Craig. *The Ministry of the Missional Church.* Grand Rapids: Baker, 2007.

Van Gelder, Craig, ed. *The Missional Church in Context: Helping Congregations Develop Contextual Ministry.* Grand Rapids: Eerdmans, 2007.

———. *The Missional Church and Leadership Formation: Helping Congregations Develop Leadership Capacity.* Grand Rapids: Eerdmans, 2009.

Walker, Andrew, and Robin Parry. *Deep Church Rising: The Third Schism and the Recovery of Christian Orthodoxy.* Eugene, OR: Cascade, 2014.

White, Newport J. D. *St. Patrick: His Writings and Life.* London: SPCK, 1920.

Whiteside, Lesley. *The Spirituality of St. Patrick.* Dublin: Columba, 1996.

Willimon, William H. "The Goal of the Seminary." *The Christian Century,* February 20, 2013, 12.

———. *How Odd of God: Chosen for the Curious Vocation of Preaching.* Louisville: Westminster/John Knox, 2015.

Wilson, Jonathan. *Living Faithfully in a Fragmented World: From After Virtue to a New Monasticism.* Eugene, OR: Cascade, 2010.

———. *Why Church Matters: Worship, Ministry and Mission in Practice.* Grand Rapids: Brazos, 2006.

Made in the USA
Lexington, KY
10 March 2019